# THE CURIOUS COLLECTOR

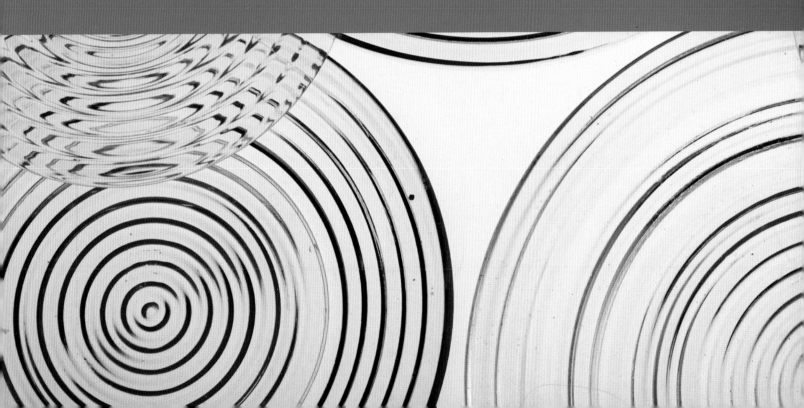

# The Curious Collector

## A Lively Little Tour of 101 Favorite Collectibles

Jessie Walker

LARK BOOKS

A Division of Sterling Publishing Co., Inc.

New York / London

**A Red Lips 4 Courage Communications, Inc. book**

www.redlips4courage.com

Eileen Cannon Paulin
*President*

Catherine Risling
*Director of Editorial*

**Book Editor:** Catherine Risling

**Contributors:** Kathleen Lavery, Lisa Sloan

**Copy Editors:** Michelle Flores, Lecia Monsen, Lori Whitcomb

**Book Designers:** Jocelyn Foye, Matt Shay

**Photographer:** Jessie Walker

**Stylists:** Aurelia Joyce Pace, Pilar Simon, Nina Williams

*Made for his sweetheart back home while resting in a foreign port, this exotic heart-shaped shell antique Sailor's Valentine is folk art.*

Library of Congress Cataloging-in-Publication Data

Walker, Jessie.
   The curious collector : a lively little tour of 101 favorite collectibles / Jessie Walker. -- 1st ed.
      p. cm.
   Includes index.
   ISBN-13: 978-1-60059-190-7 (PB-trade pbk. : alk. paper)
   ISBN-10: 1-60059-190-6 (PB-trade pbk. : alk. paper)
   1.  Collectibles--United States.  I. Title.
   NK1125.W22 2008
   790.1'32--dc22
                                     2007031528

10 9 8 7 6 5 4 3 2 1

First Edition

Published by Lark Books, A Division of
Sterling Publishing Co., Inc.
387 Park Avenue South, New York, NY 10016

Text © 2008, Jessie Walker
Photography © 2008, Jessie Walker

Distributed in Canada by Sterling Publishing,
c/o Canadian Manda Group, 165 Dufferin Street
Toronto, Ontario, Canada M6K 3H6

Distributed in the United Kingdom by GMC Distribution Services,
Castle Place, 166 High Street, Lewes, East Sussex, England BN7 1XU

Distributed in Australia by Capricorn Link (Australia) Pty Ltd.,
P.O. Box 704, Windsor, NSW 2756 Australia

If you have questions or comments about this book, please contact:
Lark Books
67 Broadway
Asheville, NC 28801
(828) 253-0467

Manufactured in China

ISBN 13: 978-1-60059-190-7
ISBN 10: 1-60059-190-6

For information about custom editions, special sales, premium and corporate purchases, please contact Sterling Special Sales Department at (800) 805-5489 or specialsales@sterlingpub.com.

# Contents

# Introduction

Have you ever wondered about all of that stuff at flea markets and antique stores? Each piece from the past—be it glassware, china, or vintage textiles—has a story behind it. On the following pages the stories of 101 of these sought-after treasures will unfold.

If you're a beginner, welcome to the world of collecting. You may be struck by the history of Depression Glass, the charm of old clocks, or the beauty of perfume bottles. Here, I help you dip into the details with photos, facts, and interesting bits of trivia. Veteran collectors, too, will discover a thing or two they may have seen before, but didn't know much about.

Like thousands of others, I love to collect. Old china plates, opaque glassware, colorful quilts, and figural cocktail shakers—I love them all and display them proudly throughout my home. I've photographed my collections—and the collections of others—for countless magazine articles and books. In the pages that follow, I share the fruits of my labors.

Let me warn you, though, there's a casual collector inside all of us. Don't be surprised if you're overcome with the urge to go on your own hunt. And once that happens, we have tips to help you get started.

## Where to Look

Antique shows devoted to one type of colectible are fun and educational. The excitement generated by bidding at an auction keeps me coming back. Flea markets hold unexpected discoveries and a chance to muse upon what life must have been like when the various objects were used.

Collecting takes on many faces. It can be visually pleasing and intellectually fascinating. If you buy on impulse, a collection will find you. Before you know it you will own three of something, which by definition is a collection.

*A perennial collector's favorite, wooden boxes displayed in a graduated stack store personal treasures.*

With more than 11,000 recognized collectibles, you might gather a treasure trove of the wildly popular Majolica pottery, or you may forge a newer category like vintage hair combs or purses. You can concentrate on a style such as Art Nouveau or Arts and Crafts; a manufacturer, perhaps Quimper, Fostoria, Hall China, or Steiff; a pattern like Fiesta, American Sweetheart, or Block Optic; or objects such as compacts or tip trays.

If you want to know more about the treasures that strike your fancy, look for books devoted to recognized antiques and collectibles by searching the Internet, your local bookstore, or antique shows. Share your passion by joining one of countless collectors groups all over the world.

## Buying Tips

There are few rules for long-term success. If you are familiar with the fine points of a collectible, you will make better choices. Always buy the best you can afford. Buy the oldest version of a particular item, as it is more likely to increase in value. If there is a choice between a teapot with a chip or one in mint condition, go for the latter.

Antique shops are usually more expensive than antique malls, but generally more choices in your specialty are available. Chat with dealers to find out if they have more of a particular collectible that may not be on display. If you're headed to an auction, it's best to examine pieces before bidding.

## Whatever You Do, Collect

The urge to collect is unrelenting. Our connection with the past feeds our desire to fill our living spaces with warmth and charm. It's what gets us up at 5 a.m. to begin our big dig for the day. It gives purpose to strolls though antique stores. And it's what fuels our passion for discovery.

*Jessie Walker*

# ceramics

········································

## chapter one

# Belleek

Belleek enjoys a faithful following among generations of families and collectors thanks to its intricately hand-painted designs and alluring iridescence.

The high-quality porcelain remains a popular choice for everyday use (tea cups, tea sets, and serviceware) and home decoration (vases and frames). A 150-year-old tradition born in an Irish town of the same name, Belleek china has made its way into folklore. According to an Irish saying, "If a newly married couple is given a gift of Belleek, the marriage will be blessed with lasting happiness."

Belleek took root in the shadow of the Irish Potato Famine. The catastrophic event of the mid-19th century saw the starvation of a quarter of the populace in Northern Ireland's County Fermanagh. When amateur mineralogist John Caldwell Bloomfield inherited the Castle Caldwell estate in 1849, including the village of Belleek, he looked for a way to generate income for himself and his tenants. After ordering a geological survey of the land, he was delighted to find that its abundant mineral wealth made fine china production a practical enterprise.

*Above:*

*The Shamrock basket, embellished with delicate flowers on its rim, is an all-time Belleek favorite still produced today.*

*Opposite:*

*The first black mark on this Belleek kettle and creamer dates the set between 1863 and 1890. The second black mark on the tea cups denotes their making between 1891 and 1926.*

## Collector's Note: Survival Technique

During World War I, Belleek made toilet bowls instead of china in order to stay in business.

When its porcelain debuted at the 1872 Dublin Exposition, the Belleek company found itself in the spotlight after Queen Victoria and the Prince of Wales made a few purchases. The china's popularity eventually led several American companies to manufacture their own versions of Irish Belleek from the 1860s until about 1930.

*This rare kettle is c. 1863–1890.*

# Identifying Marks

Belleek's first registration mark signifies the period of 1863–1890. The first mark features an Irish wolfhound craning its neck to view a castle tower; opposite the hound is a harp. Beneath this grouping is an unfurled banner with the name Belleek, flanked by small Irish shamrocks. The mark appears mostly in black, but sometimes can be found in red, orange, brown, or green.

Belleek's marking system makes it somewhat easy to date pieces, even though some patterns have been produced over a long period of time. The first three marks are black, with the last in the series ending around 1946. These were followed by three marks in green that endured until about 1980, when the gold mark came to be.

In total, there are eight markings that distinguish Belleek pieces:

- **First Mark:** Black harp, hound, and castle, 1863–1890.
- **Second Mark:** Black harp, hound, and castle and the inscription "Co. Fermanagh, Ireland," 1891–1926.
- **Third Mark:** Black, with the words "Deanta in Eirinn," 1926–1946.
- **Fourth Mark:** Green, same as the third mark except for the color, 1946–1955.
- **Fifth Mark:** Green, with an "R" inside a circle added from 1955–1965.
- **Sixth Mark:** Green, with "Co. Fermanagh" omitted between 1965–1980.
- **Seventh Mark:** Gold, with "Deanta in Eirinn" omitted between September 1980–December 1992.
- **Eighth Mark:** Blue, with a version of the second mark and an "R" inside a circle added in January 1993.

# Flow Blue

The exact origin of Flow Blue is still a mystery 200 years after catching the attention of the middle class in both England and America.

Did the unexpectedly appealing, blurry, and smudged patterns of the blue-on-white china come about through sheer chance or ingenious invention? Antique dealers and historical experts still debate whether Flow Blue started as one big mistake, but agree that further development of the blurring and smudging techniques was intentional.

British critics who ridiculed Flow Blue when it first emerged on the market quickly changed their tune when its popularity immediately soared. Flow Blue became one of the most produced ironstones—a hard, white stoneware—from its inception in the early 1800s until the early 1900s, when it finally fell out of favor.

Flow Blue is cherished for its deep royal cobalt blue, navy blue, and steel blue hues. The look is achieved when, during the glazing process, color from the transfer-printed pattern flows into the unglazed earthenware, creating the distinctive blurring. After the glazing technique was perfected, other colors such as mulberry, sepia, and dark brownish-purple emerged. Still, rich cobalt against a crisp white background remains the most desirable color combination.

*Spreading over the white surface, the color bleed hid all sorts of imperfections, from poorly joined seams to bubbles in the body of the piece.*

*Above:*

*The middle class embraced Flow Blue when it first came on the market. It was seen as affordable dinnerware that was beautiful enough to impress guests.*

*Opposite:*

*Floral patterns became popular in the 1860s and continued to attract buyers of Flow Blue into the early 20th century.*

## Spotting a Fake

If it looks different, it probably is. Check out the background on a piece of Flow Blue; if it has a greenish cast, it was made in China. Also, don't be fooled by pieces marked T. Rathbone & Co. (TR&Co); the newer insignia resembles the Victorian originals.

istorical Blue Staffordshire often takes it on the chin by being relegated to mere 19th-century ironstone transferware status. Yet artistically and culturally, it's the beloved champion in the spectrum of collectible china.

Created by English potters in the district of Staffordshire (northwest of London) specifically for export to the United States, the china patterns commonly depicted American ideals, landscapes, and lifestyles. All things Americana made up the most popular themes by far; however, collectors passionate about the scenic landscapes of foreign lands or those of bucolic farm and country life will find depictions of them readily available. These landscapes range from ancient British castles to Colonial British settlements in India, such as Fort Madurai.

The border patterns on Blue Staffordshire pieces serve as virtual signatures of the potters who designed them. Enoch Wood, for example, typically fashioned a seashell design for the border. Joseph Stubbs created a border motif that incorporated an eagle, flowers, and scrolls.

# Historical Blue Staffordshire

## Collector's Note: **Defining Ceramics**

The term *ironstone* was coined by the Mason family in England when Charles James Mason registered their Patent Ironstone China in England in 1813. Eventually 172 ironstone firms were manufacturing ironstone each with its own formula. It has come to mean a very strong ceramic.

Views of major American cities and depictions of institutional structures such as churches, banks, courthouses, hospitals, and college buildings were popular with many potters, as were scenes of battle monuments.

# Lustreware

It's easy to be seduced by the dazzling shimmer of a luster finish on pottery and porcelain.

In fact, many Lustreware enthusiasts start acquiring the colorful and often playful pieces without knowing what they are; they simply fall for the iridescent glazes.

"I'm just a sparkly kind of gal," says one New York collector who bought her first piece at a flea market more than two decades ago. "I didn't know what it was, but I thought it was gorgeous."

Tea sets are the most plentiful and popular pieces of Lustreware, which was first made by the Persians in the ninth century, followed by the Italians and the Spanish in the 15th century, the English in the 19th century, and the Czechs, Germans, and Japanese in the 20th century.

*Below:*

*Hand-painted Czechoslovakian pitchers, which came in a dozen sizes, are measuring cups for liquids.*

*Opposite:*

*The pitcher and two sugar shakers, also referred to as muffineers, are of Japanese origin, while the plates and cups are part of a Czechoslovakian snack set.*

All of the Japanese pieces, and most of the Czechoslovakian, were hand-painted. The glow and luster, most typical on the German/Bavarian pieces, come from a final glaze of sulfate that includes magnesium, iron, or zinc. These pieces were created by a lengthy multi-step process, with a transfer used as a pattern.

The styles are so diverse that many collect Lustreware by country. So distinct are some styles that it takes a keen eye and special skill to display Lustreware together, such as mixing Japanese and German/Bavarian, or Czech and German.

*The cat handle adds whimsy to an otherwise plain pitcher.*

# Majolica

Adored by Victorians yet all but forgotten by the mid-20th century, Majolica ranks once more as a fond favorite of collectors.

Many are drawn to the delightful rusticity and bright colors of this pottery that originated in the Moorish and Spanish cultures. It quickly found its way to the Spanish island of Majolica, where the pottery's clay, figuline, was abundant. The manufacture of Majolica spread across Italy, England, and America, where more than 600 factories produced it between 1850 and 1900.

Far more affordable than porcelain and bone china and bearing striking and whimsical designs, Majolica was embraced by the Victorian middle class. Plates, bowls, cups, saucers, and serving pitchers were made in a variety of naturalistic styles. Leaves, flowers, fish, and vegetables were repeated in almost endless variety.

*Vegetable and floral themes add a naturalistic quality to these Majolica serving pieces.*

Cabbages became cups, saucers, or teapots. A pitcher mimicked an ear of corn. The far-ranging imaginations of designers tweaked the public's fancy and spurred engaging conversations. Though not as valuable, reproductions are still quite appealing for their creative designs.

*Wild roses appear to climb the pitcher at right, while lily blossoms seem to cling to the cup and feathered ferns adorn the cake plates.*

## Spotting a Fake

While on the hunt for authentic Majolica, here are some things to keep in mind:

- If the lip of the pitcher doesn't allow smooth pouring, you have a reproduction rather than a genuine antique. Reproductions are meant for display rather than use.

- Modern copies usually have plain white bottoms instead of the colored or mottled base of a period piece.

- Reproductions are lighter in weight than their ancestors.

- Some contemporary copies bear historic marks, including "Etruscan Majolica" and a British registry mark. These might be reproductions, rather than fakes.

# Pickard

Pickard set the gold standard as a producer of fine china in more ways than one. Since its founding in Wisconsin more than a century ago, the company has decorated each of its pieces with actual gold.

This trademark move means that it's virtually impossible to find a Pickard plate, cup, or saucer without gold. Now run by fifth-generation family members, Pickard serves as the official china of the U.S. State Department and its embassies and consulates throughout the world, not to mention several major hotel chains.

The most desirable Pickard—which are also the most scarce—are turn-of-the-century and early 21st-century pieces individually signed by craftsmen brought from Europe to decorate the china. On top of the most-wanted list are the works of master German painter Paul Gasper and Jeremiah Vokal, who emigrated from Prague and painted captivating grape patterns on large gold-rimmed goblets. Ohio-born Curtis Marker painted white dogwood on gold-trimmed vases, while Florence James, an especially talented artist known for many motifs, painted Dutch designs.

The Pickard blank is marked with either the Limoges or Haviland symbol. During World War I, Pickard imported blanks from Japan and also bought them from American potteries. Some collectors prefer Pickard's scenic paintings, while others are drawn to images of people, birds, animals, and flowers. Collections can be assembled by theme, artist, or period, but expect the earliest Pickard pieces to be the most challenging to find.

*Below:*

*The chrysanthemum floral theme comes alive on the large vase and the perfume bottles. These early pieces are not signed.*

*Opposite:*

*Five different artists painted these pictorial vases with a style that is most definitely Pickard. The peacock vase is by Edward Challinor. The woman and dog are by F. Cinarcty. The hunting dogs are by Otto Podlaha and the slender water lily vase is by Leach.*

# Quimper

This hand-painted, tin-glazed earthenware has been in continuous production in the town of Quimper in Brittany, France, for more than 300 years.

Quimper stands out for the richly colored and highly detailed illustrations of everyday village life painted by hand on larger pieces, such as platters. Collectors admire the charming Breton peasant who made his first appearance in the late 1800s on scores of pieces. Also well known is the Breton marriage scene that shows a wedding party leaving the church after the ceremony. The names of villages and their crests often were painted on plates.

*Top:*

*A typical Breton peasant in a costume of the late 1800s decorates the center of this antique plate.*

*Left:*

*This plate features both the name of the town where it was made and its crest on the outer rim.*

## Collector's Note: **Price Pointer**

A more colorful rendition of the petite Breton peasant, a fluted border, and a richly decorated border typically indicate a higher value of a Quimper plate.

# Spongeware

Imagine this pitch in an advertising circular: "No sparing of the sponge on this pottery." So true, and yet when it comes to Spongeware, it's so signature. The stamped design tends to be a bit blurry and the spacing uneven, defining Spongeware's handmade look and charm. Many collectors use the terms Spatterware and Spongeware interchangeably, yet there are clear differences.

First made in late 18th-century Scotland, Spatterware boasts designs created by the tapping of a brush loaded with paint against the heavy-paste earthenware.

Spongeware, a less expensive earthenware, was produced in 19th-century England, Scotland, Ireland, Wales, and the United States. Its stamped patterns were achieved by dabbing color and designs on the pottery with a cloth or a sponge. A cut sponge attached to a stick was often used to fashion Spongeware's decorative forms, among them flowers and diamond shapes.

Because Spongeware was created for utilitarian purposes, few pieces are without some chips, cracks, or crazing. These signs of wear don't lower the value. In fact, the earthenware has enjoyed renewed popularity, with handsome new Spongeware widely available on the market.

Collector's Note: **Ringing True**

Listen while you thump your fingernail on a piece of Spongeware. The most highly fired will produce a ringing sound, while areas with less firing will produce a dull thud.

# Staffordshire Spaniels

These sweet spaniels look just as charming on today's mantels as they did during the mid-Victorian era, when they were at the height of their popularity.

Becoming a collector of these cuddly canines requires specific knowledge and a good eye. The essential skill needed is learning how to distinguish the old from the new and the best from the ordinary. Since the Staffordshire Spaniels were hand-painted, no two will look exactly alike. The quality of paint varies greatly in these pieces.

Red or rust and white dogs are the most plentiful, followed by black-and-white, all-white, and jet black dogs known as Jackfields. Dogs carrying baskets are more difficult to find, while Staffordshire Spaniels smoking pipes are the most rare of all.

If the piece is hollow cast, it is a later piece. Figurines with flat backs came after those with rounded backs. Staffordshire Spaniels were originally made in pairs, but it's much easier for collectors to find single dogs than a near-perfect match.

# Stoneware

Fans of no-nonsense Stoneware appreciate country-style, salt-glazed pottery that is as unpretentious as it is lovely.

This durable, waterproof ware originated in 15th-century Germany. It was introduced in the United States during the colonial era and became the dominant houseware in the young republic from 1790 until 1890.

Stoneware's qualities fall midway between earthenware and porcelain. It is highly fired to the point where vitrification makes it incapable of being penetrated, thus making Stoneware ideal for storing food and liquids.

In the last half of the 19th century, potters in New York and New England began creating Stoneware figurines, applying a whimsical style to dogs, deer, birds, elephants, flowers, houses, and other motifs. To create the Stoneware look, a dark gray solution of clay, water, and the extremely expensive cobalt blue oxide is painted on the unfired pieces. During the firing process, the cobalt reacts to the iron oxide to produce the vibrant decoration.

*Because stoneware is nonporous, glaze is applied only for decoration.*

# Tea Leaf

How a tea leaf unfolds at the bottom of a cup is said to be a harbinger of fortune. No wonder, then, that the tea leaf became such a popular motif in copper luster glazed pottery.

The motif evolved into many patterns (with names like Teaberry, Pepper, and Pre-Leaf) that were applied to the outside of more than 150 body styles in copper luster. The production of Tea Leaf ironstone started more than 150 years ago, shortly after the English potter Anthony Shaw registered his designs in 1856.

The manufacture of Tea Leaf spread to three dozen potteries in Britain and two dozen in America. It became known as the "common folks" china, as this durable ironstone was less expensive than fine bone china and porcelain. It is resistant to chips, cracks, and crazing.

*Right:*

*The tea set is an 1843 pre-Tea Leaf variant in a Rococo shape made by Bridgewood & Sons. Today's collectors have expanded the definition of Tea Leaf to include white china decorated with any copper luster motif.*

*Opposite:*

*The covered butter dish (far left) is by Meakin, and the two handleless cups are by Elsmore and Roster.*

Dawn Stolzfus and Jeffrey Snyder, authors of "White Ironstone, A Survey of Its Many Forms," note that ironstone was "harder than earthenware and stronger than porcelain."

Despite its popularity, its everyday use waned in the early 1900s. But, some would believe, luck is on the side of the enthusiast who acquires a rare specimen of this highly collectible ironstone.

Collector's Note:
**Spotting Repairs**
. . . . . . . . . . . . . . . . . . . . . . . . . . . . .
A repaired teapot lid does not lower the value of an otherwise perfect tea set. You can see even the most skillfully executed repair if you hold the piece up to a bright light.

*Tea Leaf pattern ironstone made by various manufacturers including J. & G. Meakin, William Adams, Barrow & Co., and Bridgewater & Clarke line an antique pine cabinet.*

# Toby Jugs

With such jovial expressions, who can resist these fun jugs and mugs?

Toby jugs have been around for almost 300 years. Typically, they are character jugs (or mugs) depicting a jovial man in 19th-century clothing wearing a three-cornered hat and holding a jug of beer and/or a glass or pipe. The pointed tricorn allows convenient pours from the jug.

*Grouping Toby jugs by size creates an effective display.*

In the 19th century, Royal Daulton developed a wide range of character jugs. Considering the jolly grins and unique expressiveness of these vessels, it's easy to see why vintage pieces are sought after and reproductions are popular.

### Collector's Note: **Defects That Devalue**
. . . . . . . . . . . . . . . . . . . . . . . . . . . . . . .
A broken finger is considered a minor blemish. If an arm is missing or the base has been shattered and repaired, point out these defects to the dealer and ask to pay a lower price.

# Watt Pottery

For most collectors, the search for a prized piece is half the fun. For Watt Pottery collectors, few finds are as heady as coming across a rare pitcher.

Increase your enjoyment of Watt by learning its patterns, such as Apple, Pansy (sometimes called Wild Rose), Dutch Tulip, Morning Glory, Starflower, Eagle, and Rooster. All have a dark cream background decorated with hand-painted designs in bold reds and greens. The patterns blend well, creating an appealing grouping on a shelf or in a bookcase. And since most Watt

Pottery was meant for kitchen use, why not put them on display in the kitchen?

Watt Pottery was manufactured by the Watt Pottery Company. They began production in 1922 and closed in 1965 after a fire destroyed their factory and warehouse. Apple was a popular series and is the most sought-after of all of the designs. Creamers are perhaps the most difficult pieces to find. Advertising for various companies appears on numerous pieces, and so many design variations were made without a pattern name.

# Wedgwood

Collectors with a taste for more formal and delicate tableware simply adore Wedgwood.

Many collectors and experts consider the names Jasperware and Wedgwood synonymous. This beautiful ceramic pottery with a white or colored stoneware body was invented in 1775. It is the master accomplishment of Josiah Wedgwood and is named for the semi-precious stone, jasper.

Wedgwood is made from translucent stoneware clay that marries barium sulphate with Wedgwood formulas to produce its dense matte finish. Thin white relief portraits of Greek classical scenes, called cameos, are attached to the surface.

The model for the first important piece of Wedgwood came from the Portland Vase, named for its British owners of the last 200 years. Although experts do not agree, scenes on the vase and the style of work date this vessel to between 20 B.C. and the year 100.

*With little interruption, shapes and designs like these have been produced from 1790 until today.*

The scene on the Portland Vase most seen in photographs has been interpreted as either the Emperor Augustus' supposed siring by the god Apollo in the form of a snake or Mark Anthony being lured by the wiles of Cleopatra.

## Spotting a Fake

Copies of Wedgwood were made in Germany during the late 1920s. If the outline of the white figures is blurred rather than crisp and the base or back lacks an incised Wedgwood mark, the piece is a reproduction rather than one made by Wedgwood's Ethuria Pottery.

*Left:*

*Most famous of all, the Portland Vase was first manufactured by Wedgwood in 1790. This one is c. 1964.*

*Opposite:*

*Used primarily for decoration on mantels or cabinets, the c. 1860 covered urn is part of a garniture set, which has the same embossing designs on a group. An online search shows countless antiques advertised as garniture sets. The miniature cup is highly collectible because it is so rare.*

# glass

·········································

## chapter two

# American Sweetheart

A slow movie night might offer a prize dish to each ticket holder. Someone buying dining room furniture at a local store might receive a whole set of glassware.

The much-loved pink American Sweetheart glass is probably followed in popularity by the highly opalescent, almost transparent white Monax, both developed by MacBeth Evans Glass Company.

American Sweetheart, which was manufactured from 1930 to 1936, has never been reproduced. MacBeth Evans was bought by Corning Glass Works of New York in 1937.

*Right:*

*The painted decoration was probably added after this Monax dinner plate left the factory.*

*Opposite:*

*American Sweetheart, a mold-etched glass, was offered as a premium in boxes of oats or bags of flour.*

The rather complex mold-etched pattern described as festoons with ribbons and a scroll design with a scalloped edge brought elegance to the table during grim times. Mass-produced, it was available in dime stores and as giveaways and premiums. It may take years to find all of the items in the 33-piece set of American Sweetheart.

While American Sweetheart could easily be found at flea markets, antique malls, or estate sales at one time, now your best bet is to visit special glass shows or search online.

Collector's Note: **What is Monax?**

Monax was created by the MacBeth Evans Glass Company. The white glass was originally developed for light fixtures. In 1933, MacBeth Evans began using it in their tableware. By then, their products' delicate designs were quite strong and resilient.

*This stack features a delicate pink sugar bowl, cereal bowls, tumblers, and a cup and saucer.*

# Cranberry Glass

Cranberry glass was cherished during the Victorian era when almost every household item that could be made in glass was produced in cranberry colors.

The nearly transparent yellow-red cranberry glass (resembling the color of cranberry juice) has been made in America and Europe since the Civil War. It was a favorite of consumers and collectors from early on for its wonderfully shimmering, ruby-like sheen. The enchanting hue is obtained with difficulty, requiring exact amounts of the gold chloride that is mixed into the molten glass base.

*This c. 1850 ceiling fixture has been electrified. The ring of flat glass at the top is a smoke bell to keep the ceiling clean in the days when candles were used in this fixture.*

Old pieces include vases, pitchers, decanters, bowls, perfume bottles, plates, stemware, and more, and can be dated by their shape. Short scroll legs on bowls, twisted handles on jugs, glass beads added to the surface, and baskets of all kinds were the rage in the late 1800s. New pieces have shapes all their own, and both old and new are considered collectible.

Beware, though, crude reproductions are out there. Look for reputable sellers, such as the A.A. Importing Company, that offer catalogs filled with reproductions of glass accessories, including cranberry glass.

## Spotting a Fake

Reproductions of cranberry glass are rife. These pieces are usually heavier and can be noted for their poor craftsmanship. If they have a bluish-purple tint, copper may have been substituted for gold during the manufacturing process. There are quality new pieces being made today in shapes different from the old.

*Right:*

*This vintage 1930s pitcher was probably used as a vase.*

*Opposite:*

*Victorian wine decanters had both cranberry and clear-glass stoppers like the one pictured here.*

# Fenton Glass

You can't help but give the Fenton Art Glass Company credit for exercising imitation as the sincerest form of flattery.

Its admiration for the iridescent beauty of Tiffany and Stuben prompted the company to invent its own comparable line of glassware that's known today as Carnival glass.

As America's largest manufacturer of handmade colored glass, Fenton offers much more than the wildly popular Carnival. The company, which got its start in 1905, also introduced lines such as Hobnail, Ruffle, and Crest to a public eager for imaginative designs and bright colors. Fenton's knack for keeping its finger on the pulse of public demand spurred the production of formal vases, urns, bowls, pitchers, plates, and other glassware in a wide variety of shapes and dazzling colors.

*Below:*

*Glass signs caught the public's attention at Fenton point-of-purchase displays.*

*Opposite:*

*Fenton is known for its transparent and lightly tinted crystal and densely colored opalescent glass. The Curtain Optic pattern pictured here came on the market in 1927.*

The company's deft creativity also is seen in its transparent to lightly tinted crystal, densely colored opalescent glass, and stretch glass, which has an iridescent surface.

Founded by Frank L. Fenton and his brother, John W. Fenton, in an old glass factory in Ohio, the company initially used blanks from other glass manufacturers to produce its wares. Before too long, the brothers decided to produce their own glass to make sure they had the stock they needed to invent new colors and designs. In 1907, Fenton moved to Williamstown, West Virginia, where it has been in continuous production ever since.

It's believed that there are 130 patterns in Carnival glass. Inspired by the popular milk glass of the 1950s, the company created a white Hobnail glass, which is distinguished by its all-over raised dots, that became a best seller.

*Pictured here is a 1920s opalescent Swirl pattern sugar and a Blue Ridge pitcher.*

# Etched Glass

Fine tables around the world have sparkled for centuries with dazzling pieces of etched glass. In fact, many beautiful examples dating back to early Roman times are on display in museums throughout the world.

The tools used to craft these historic pieces died with the civilizations that created them and remain undiscovered. Experts agree that the finest form of glass engraving today comes from the copper wheel, which allows for true cutting.

*A large cut crystal vase c. 1920 stands behind a large carafe c. 1880 with a delicately etched bubble stopper. The pair of wine glasses c. 1920 is decorated with a grape and leaf pattern.*

# Jadeite

When it comes to Jadeite, you just can't get hung up on the spelling of this collectible.

This Depression-era glassware, developed by the McKee Glass Company in 1930, can be found online under several spellings: Jade-ite, Jad-ite, Jadeite, and Jadite.

For years, Jadeite flew under the radar in the collectibles market, being easy to find and inexpensive to buy at flea markets and swap meets. After American domestic doyenne Martha Stewart announced her love for the enchanting machine-made translucent glass (both on her TV show and in her magazine), prices took off.

Jadeite was produced in such large quantities during the Depression era that it was often given away for free. Buy a few gallons of gasoline for your automobile and receive a new piece to add to your colorful set of dinner dishes.

*Right:*
*This Jadeite cup and saucer are striking in their simplicity.*

*Opposite:*
*Jadeite's refreshing shades of green vary in hue and transparency from one manufacturer to another. The Jane Ray pattern pieces on the right are a different shade of green and are not as translucent as the cup and saucer above.*

American companies such as the Jeannette Glass Company and Anchor Hocking (produced under the latter's Fire-King division) applied advanced automation technology in the manufacture of Jadeite. Anchor Hocking made the vast majority of the glassware from about 1945 to 1975.

These days, the green glass is being reproduced in foreign countries. Anchor Hocking maintains the integrity of its reproduction patterns by producing it in a different color and size.

Collector's Note:
### Reproductions in Circulation
A new cup and saucer/plate (no ring on the plate) in a lighter green than Fire King's original Laurel pattern Jadeite is available. This reproduction is marked with a diamond on the bottom numbered 402 and 4.

*These stacked cups feature the Jane Ray pattern.*

# Manhattan

Forty years after ending production of Manhattan glassware, Anchor Hocking capitalized on the popularity of its Art Deco-inspired concentric ribs with a look-alike pattern he dubbed Park Avenue.

Hocking made Manhattan between 1938–1943. It debuted Park Avenue in 1987, producing it until 1993, then again briefly in the late 1990s.

Casual collectors don't seem to mind the similar pieces, according to glass expert Gene Florence. Perhaps that's because Hocking maintained the integrity of the old glass by altering the sizes, shapes, and colors of the new pattern.

Those who want to know the difference can check the sizes of genuine Manhattan in Florence's "Collector's Encyclopedia of Depression Glass." For example, the Manhattan glass tray measures 14", while the Park Avenue tray measures 13".

Manhattan bowls are just under 2" tall while Park Avenue bowls measure over 2". The Manhattan Berry Bowl is slightly larger than the cereal bowl, which has no handles and sells for three times the price.

*Manhattan doesn't resemble what most think of as Depression Glass, which is associated with fancy edges and a delicate design. While rubbing fingers across the ribs, a little ting will be heard if it is real.*

Sometimes Heisey's Ridgeleigh glass has been mistaken for Manhattan. It has the same appealing Art Deco look, but one should expect to pay more for Heisey as it is more collectible.

If you like a particular piece well enough to pay the price, go for it. Some collectors want to know a lot about what they are accumulating, while others simply enjoy the thrill of the hunt and surrounding themselves with pieces that give them an emotional high.

*Left and Opposite:*

*Crystal is the most common Manhattan glass color. Pink, ruby, green, and iridescent were also made but pink is the most difficult to find, with cups being especially elusive. If you happen on a pale blue piece it is Park Avenue and not Manhattan.*

# Mercury Glass

There's nothing like the sublimely mirrored surface and silvery shine of Mercury glass, hence its appeal. No wonder old pieces are in high demand and modern reproductions abound.

The introduction of Mercury glass occurred almost simultaneously in Bohemia, England, and the United States, and created a sensation. It was produced in the latter half of the 19th century and into the first few decades of the 20th century.

Bohemian glass is the easiest to find, as it was made in the largest quantities of the three from 1840 until about 1920. Made with soda lime, Bohemian glass is lighter than its English and American cousins, which were made with flint lead glass. Being heavier, the English and American glass could withstand engraving.

Silvered doorknobs were the first use of Mercury glass, followed by religious statuary, compotes, drapery tiebacks, beakers, gazing globes, vases, candlesticks, goblets, pitchers, and Christmas tree ornaments. Decorating was a fast-growing cottage industry in Europe and as a result, many items made with Mercury glass show an astounding variety of techniques and patterns. Styles range from the elegant to the brightly colored to the austerely simple.

# Milk Glass

Milk glass originally was known as opal glass until someone got the idea that the glass resembled the cool opaqueness of milk.

It was intended to look like porcelain and Victorians seized upon the glassware as a more affordable alternative to porcelain tableware. Perhaps because purity is associated with the color white, milk glass was used in the production of cosmetic and toiletry bottles from the 1870s into the 1920s.

This mass-produced glass tableware was a wonderful substitute for the more costly European glass and china, but its popularity waned after World War I.

Despite its creation as a color-less glass (that is, defined by manufacturers as having an absence of color), milk glass can be found in colors other than white, including blue, green, yellow, pink, brown, and even black. And shades of white abound. But no matter the color, genuine milk glass glows with a milky opalescence.

*Milk glass candlesticks are available in an almost endless variety of designs.*

Buying a two-piece set such as a jar and lid can be tricky. The lid and cover should fit well and be of the same color. If they are loose they were not manufactured as a set, but put together later. Collectors call this making a marriage. Two parts that were made by different manufacturers and then put together are called a mixed marriage. Sometimes Westmoreland pieces have a number on both the lid and the base. If these numbers match, it is a perfect fit.

---

Collector's Note: **Guess Its Age**

Because the wonderful old molds for making milk glass have been transferred from company to company, it is almost impossible to identify the age of a milk glass piece by its shape. Some collectors believe a foolproof indicator of old glass is its opalescence at the edges. Many older pieces of milk glass share this trait, but not all. New glass carries the same quality of opalescence.

---

*Left:*

*Opaque white milk glass hit the zenith of its popularity at the close of the 19th century.*

*Opposite:*

*This stack of dishes represents crimped edge, open lace edge, closed lattice edge, and beaded edge designs. The pitcher is the plentiful Hobnail design.*

# Rose Bowls

Delicate glass orbs with top edges that are turned in and crimped reigned as must-have accessories in the Victorian home.

The containers, ranging from 4½"–7½" in diameter and featuring etched designs or cutwork, were used to hold potpourri (better to freshen the heavily draped parlors of the day where musty velour fabrics captured stale pipe smoke). The bowls were filled halfway with Gallica rose petals and set on a sunlit shelf so that the beautiful glass would catch the light in spectacular fashion.

Though plentiful more than 100 years ago, rose bowls are scarce today. For those who love the look but fail to find a vintage piece, an ample supply of reproductions by Italian as well as American glass makers such as Fenton are widely available.

Reproductions are collectible, but the past few decades have seen batches enter the secondary market as vintage pieces. New collectors should take care not to be fooled. The removal of the Murano sticker from a high-quality piece of Italian glass is all it takes sometimes to confuse vintage and modern pieces.

*Right:*
*Rose bowls can be either transparent or translucent.*

*Opposite:*
*Quilted diamond (left) and herringbone are some of the more popular rose bowl patterns.*

Copies commonly have anywhere from five to 12 crimps. Authentic rose bowls usually show an even number of crimps, most often six, but sometimes eight or 12. The Italian reproductions frequently are pointed, uneven, or a bit square. True vintage pieces have crimps that are softly rounded and flow from one to another.

## Spotting a Fake

The Italians produced beautiful reproductions of Victorian rose bowls beginning in the 1960s. Thicker glass distinguishes the Italian copies. The newer pieces are gritty to the touch in contrast to the silky feel of the 100-year-old bowls.

*Some collectors specialize in Souvenir bowls like these from the 1893 World's Fair. Travel destinations are sometimes featured on the original rose bowls.*

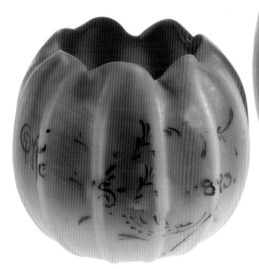

# Sandwich Glass

Beginning collectors will find the term Sandwich Glass used to identify two distinct categories of glassware.

Sandwich Glass refers to the 1820s–1880s glassware made by the Boston & Sandwich Glass Co., Cape Cod Glassworks, and other companies located in and around the town of Sandwich, Massachusetts.

Sandwich Glass also refers to glassware patterns inspired by those that originated in the 19th century, created by a number of companies from the 1920s to the present.

If you're a purist on the hunt for original 19th-century Sandwich Glass, consult a reference dictionary or search online for identification and appraisal resources. The patterns made popular by the original glassmakers in Sandwich feature a flower and ornate scroll motif. The space between the designs is filled with stippling (tiny raised dots).

*Pressed-glass containers were produced for numerous household uses. Both the amethyst Twisted Loop pattern and the blue Loop pattern vases have gauffered rims.*

Refinement of the pressing process broke American dependence on hand-blown or hand-pressed English glass. The Sandwich Glass Company developed a method of pressing molten glass into molds, thus creating the first mass-produced glassware. It was more affordable and the fine quality made it an attractive alternative to cut or engraved glass.

What makes Sandwich Glass an appealing collectible is its wide range of patterns that are still available. More than 1,500 patterns were made in the United States, with nearly half making up an entire setting.

Collectors of newer Sandwich Glass, referred to as "pattern glass," can find a majority of these pieces—from goblets to pitchers to vases—at affordable prices.

*Below:*

*The Peacock Eye Shield Tray was the bottom of a two-piece set that dates between 1835 and 1845.*

*Opposite:*

*Candlesticks, vases, and salt dishes like these without covers were indispensable to the 19th-century table. Small spoons were used to distribute the salt.*

# metals

......................................................

## chapter three

# Advertising Tins

Once purchased for their contents, vintage tins make a colorful collection, giving your home a nostalgic, kitschy feel.

There was a time when tins stored everything from coffee, pretzels, and syrup to medicines, motor oil, cigars, and pencils. That means collectors can hunt down their tin treasures two different ways: by brand or by what was originally inside.

The first advertising tins made their debut when English printer Ben George George (yes, that's his name) improved the process of transfer printing and joined Victorian designer Owen Jones to create ornate containers for Huntley & Palmer, supplier of biscuits (cookies) to the Royal Family household. Soon ornamental tins of all shapes and sizes were popping up. Like tiny works of art, they picture everything from hot air balloons to men playing chess to horse-drawn carriages.

*Right:*

*Turn-of-the-last-century spice tins display images ranging from the comic strip character Buster Brown (1900–1910) to the Happy Homemaker, Mother Dawson.*

*Opposite:*

*These British advertising tins are at least 100 years old.*

Tins today can pull double duty, holding household items while cheering up a room. If the tin you bring home is dirty, just give it a gentle wash with clear water and wipe it dry with a soft cloth.

Canisters may be round, pie-shaped, or square. Metal lunch boxes are made with one or two handles. Tins bore paper labels before lithography was successfully printed directly on the metal. Lids included knobs, snap down features, and hinged closures.

## Spotting a Fake

If the design is intricate but the colors are fresh and bold, the advertising tin is a reproduction rather than vintage. The colors of antique tins are usually a tad faded. Much lighter metal is also used in copies.

*Artwork dominates British biscuit tins, sometimes with little or no mention of its content; American tins describe what's inside.*

# Flower Frogs

Thankfully, hunting down these interesting frogs won't give you warts.

Flower frogs got their name because they sit in water while holding flower arrangements. The first patent for a metal flower frog (others are made of porcelain and glass) was issued in 1916. Housewives eager to dress up their dinner tables gobbled them up.

But the frogs really took off in the 1930s when the floral industry began delivering arrangements and needed them to stay put during transit. Thousands of designs were created during the flower frog heyday, which lasted until the '50s, just as the June Cleaver era was winding down. It took modern-day June Cleaver, Martha Stewart, to resurrect the frog craze with regular flower arranging sessions on her TV show.

*Lead frogs and turtles are abundant forms.*

Vintage flower frogs are made of wire, stainless steel, brass, copper, aluminum, cast iron, and lead. Some might be a bit rusty, others painted green.

These metal holders were originally referred to as flower bricks, blocks, arrangers, or holders. The 1940s slang term, flower frog, has become the accepted phrase used for a flower arranger today.

Collector's Note:
**If it's good enough for a Kennedy...**
Eleven metal flower frogs from the estate of Jacqueline Bouvier Kennedy Onassis brought $4,025 at auction in 1996.

*Left:*

*These green metal frog flower holders are adjustable.*

*Opposite:*

*Metal frog holders were made in a great variety of shapes.*

# French
# Enamel

If a magazine spread of a French cottage kitchen makes you feel all warm and fuzzy inside, then enamelware just might be the collection for you.

Charming French enamel is coveted for its glossy pastel palette: baby blues, old-fashioned pinks, bright aquas, and warm creams. Authentic pieces often have hairline "age" cracks, giving them character.

The milk pitchers, long-handled pots, canisters, and sieves you can find today at antique stores and flea markets once brightened kitchens throughout Europe, so they ought to look used.

The French began manufacturing enamel-ware in the late 1800s by painting metal and cast iron kitchen items with multiple coats of enamel and then firing them to bake on the finish, giving them a glassy, glossy look and protecting them from rusting.

*Right:*

*The double-handled coffee pot, called a "biggin" after its inventor, M. Biggin of France, dates back to the early 1800s and is manufactured in large quantities today.*

*Opposite:*

*The botanical and graphic designs air-brushed onto many pieces were considered a legitimate art form at the time.*

Each factory guarded its slightly different enamel formula. Sometimes after the work was fired at least 820c (1508f) and polished, a final layer of clear enamel was added. Japy Freres & Company invented a stamp press, triggering mass production.

Traveling in France, collectors can begin their search for enamelware in the magazine, *Aladdin*, available on any Paris newsstand.

Collector's Note:
**Designed & Dated**
● ● ● ● ● ● ● ● ● ● ● ● ● ● ● ● ● ● ● ● ●
If you're lucky enough to find a piece of French enamel with an original label, which will help to date the piece, you'll have a much more valuable piece.

*Trimmed in black and white, a child's cup sits with a canister set in yellow and white with a touch of red. Canisters are collectors' favorites.*

# French Tole

What started as a commercial enterprise, French tole is now a classic collector's item with an old-world feel.

In the 1700s, art schools began training apprentices in what was called a one-stroke style of painting. With a single stroke of a brush (loaded with multiple colors of oil paint), the apprentice could decorate a tea tray or a lamp with a bird, a butterfly, or a piece of fruit. It was purely commercial. The quicker the items were painted and ready for sale, the more money there was to be made. As a result, there's a lot of tole out there for a collector to track down, although some of the more rare 18th-century pieces can fetch a considerable amount.

Black, yellow, mustard, green, red, and cream are the most often used background colors for French tole metal ware, and many pieces are gilded. Collectors can find tole on candleholders, tea caddies, trays, plates, watering cans, baskets, and all sorts of bedroom accessories.

It's believed that the art form got its name because, way back when, a tea tray used to be called a tea board. The French word for board is tole. Tea tray painters then were probably called tole painters.

*The sage green tole basket with handle, c. 1930, is decorated with a floral design and gilding.*

It's a good idea to use a magnifying glass for a careful study of an item to see if the design is painted. A combination of transfer and paint was frequently used from 1920 until about 1930. A sign of wear might be a good thing, as the item is less likely to be a clever reproduction if it looks used.

*Below:*

*Florals were the most used decorating theme when this butter yellow tea caddy was made in the early 1900s.*

*Above:*

*Lovely hand-painted florals dominate the design of this 1880 antique sage green French tole basket.*

*Opposite:*

*Letters are clustered in a cream 1900 jardinière, while the antique sage green waste can is used as a flower container.*

### Collector's Note: **Artist's Insight**

Both the body and shadow of a leaf or flower on French tole pieces are created in one stroke with a paintbrush loaded with several colors. This technique was developed to decorate more quickly. Oil paint was, and still is, the medium used.

# Graniteware

Back in the late 1800s, American women prized graniteware for its light weight and easy cleaning. Today they snap it up for its country-kitchen charm.

Graniteware is splattered enamelware. Enamelware (enamel-covered iron) was first mass-produced in Europe in the late 19th century. Artisan immigrants arrived on American shores with the secret formulas and then proceeded to put their own spin on it.

Instead of just coating pots and pans in solid colors, they threw in white swirls or speckles. Collectors can still find colorful vintage coffee pots, ladles, mugs, bread tins, buckets, jelly molds, and strainers.

Graniteware supposedly got its name from Granite Iron Ware, one of the first lines produced in America in 1876 by the St. Louis Stamping Co. Stamps on the bottom of pieces help provide identification. Some might be stamped *Made in Yugoslavia #3, Made in England, DRU Holland,* or *Cream City Ware, G&P&F, Milwaukee.*

*Above and Opposite:*

*Collectors usually concentrate on graniteware made between 1870 and 1940. If you like the look and can't afford the old, you could go for the newer, lighter weight graniteware made from the 1970s on, or even the reproductions that are being imported today.*

## Spotting a Fake
• • • • • • • • • • • • • • • • • • • • • • • • • • • • • • • •
Today's manufacturers are reproducing everything from children's tea sets to coffee boilers. Reproductions from Asia, Mexico, and Europe with dents and signs of wear, to make them look old, are exported every day. Collector's guides contain photographs and detailed information about the real deal.

# Hotel Silver

A longing for the days when elegant travel meant fresh white linens topped with gleaming silver services is what drives the collector of hotel silver.

Collectors and dealers alike appreciate the glamour of a bygone era when each meal course was served with the correct flatware, such as a fruit or fish knife, and when finger bowls were a must.

Clean lines and stamped insignia distinguish hotel silver. Pieces include everything associated with food and beverage service. Treasure hunters can expect to find plates, platters, entree domes, champagne buckets, wine coolers, sugar tongs, pickle forks, finger bowls, butter tubs, and dessert forks.

The appealing patina developed through a hundred years of polishing heightens the charm of this sought-after collectible. Some look for the insignia that reveals their former use at the Ritz Hotel in Paris, the Plaza in New York, the Excelsior in Rome, or perhaps the Connaught in London. Other pieces started out on a luxury ocean liner or a train.

# Ice Cream Molds

It turns out that the Victorians liked their ice cream as much as we do. But instead of stuffing it into cones, they squished their hand-cranked ice cream into heavy pewter molds.

Back in the Middle Ages, ice cream, along with pudding, were desserts that symbolized sophistication and status. There were no ice cream shops back then, so people with means made it at home. Collectors, though, are warned that they should no longer actually use the vintage molds they find because of the lead content. Antique molds are now only for display.

You can find ice cream molds in hundreds of designs, ranging from angels and fruit to George Washington, cupid, Mother Goose, and Father Christmas.

*Banquet-size bird and train molds are pictured with an individual-size rider on a horse.*

Most ice cream molds are two parts and stamped with the manufacturer's initials along with the style or design number of the mold. A double "C" indicates a French manufacturer. "L.G." stands for the most well known of the German makers. There were also the big three American makers—"E & Co., NY," which stands for Eppelsheimer & Company; "S & Co." for Schall & Co.; and "K & Co." for Krauss. Pewter molds were typically made in two sizes: individual (single-portion) and banquet (10" or larger).

A novice collector might want to start with a theme in mind, say Teddy bears or trains. It is not as easy to find ice cream molds at flea or antique markets as it was a few years back. The Internet has a lot to offer, and can even lead you to a London store that has 2,000 pieces in stock.

*Left:*

*Pictured is a representative group of the endless designs used for pewter ice cream molds. Most of these are the individual size.*

*Opposite:*

*The style of the hinge helps identify the manufacturer.*

# Match Safes

What began as a practical contraption to safely carry your matches and provide a surface to strike that match on has evolved into tiny works of art.

During their relatively short life, from the mid-1800s to World War II, hundreds of match safes were designed in all manner of fascinating and sometimes funny shapes. You might find a geisha, a hand, or a cowboy boot in your search.

For the wealthy folk, there were match safes made of silver, gold, and platinum. Others were decorated with enamel pictures of manly things (since most smokers were men) like a turkey, soldier, or naked lady.

*Right:*

*The shoe match safe is Austrian silver c. 1890, while the oblong safe is European silver c. 1890.*

*Opposite:*

*Gold match safes, decorated with jewels, were made by Cartier and Tiffany.*

The safes took on a second job: besides holding matches, they were ice-breakers that were often good for a few laughs.

The safes that fetch the most money today were made with exotic materials like jade, tortoiseshell, and ivory, and sometimes bejeweled with precious gems.

### Collector's Note:
### Vestas in Thousands

Match safes, or *vestas* as they are called in Great Britain, were manufactured in thousands of designs worldwide.

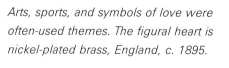

*Arts, sports, and symbols of love were often-used themes. The figural heart is nickel-plated brass, England, c. 1895.*

# Antique Scales

There's a saying: Old scale collectors never die, they just lose their balance.

It is fascinating to learn not only the purpose of the scales you collect, but also who made them, how they work, and the time and place where they were used.

The Romans made scales 3,000 years ago. But probably the most popular for collectors are postal scales. The oldest of these date to the British Uniform Postal Act of 1840.

You can also find toy scales or scales made specifically to weigh eggs, coins, or candy. Opium scales from the Orient were used for medicine, spices, gems, and gold. The beams on these are made of ivory, the pan of brass and occasionally silver.

Depending on what the scale was made for, it will have a different design. The pendulum scale has a weight fixed to an arm that swings upward when a load is being weighed. The spring scale uses springs to balance the load being weighed. The platform scale employs a system of levers, below the platform, which transfer the load to the weighing resistance, no matter where the load is placed on the platform.

*Cast-iron candy store scales once sat on the counter of small shops.*

The manufacturer's registered logos stamped on the bottom of most scales are loaded with information, such as the name of the company, model number, date of the scale, and the patent number.

*This bean scale is the same design that was used in 6000 B.C. to measure gold dust.*

# Antique Silver

Antique silver is one of the oldest of collectibles and can fulfill many a fancy.

There are antique silver candlesticks, pitchers, holy water fonts, ashtrays, candle snuffers, pill boxes, and spoons lurking at estate sales and flea markets. You can also collect your silver by country, choosing only pieces from Germany, Russia, or Colonial America.

Silversmiths were often inspired by animals. Horses, lions, and serpents decorate serving pieces, knives, and handles.

A piece of old silver will often tell you something about its original owner. Some bear an inscription or family crest. Before 1800 in the United Kingdom, everything from mugs to coffee pots bore a coat of arms to represent its nobility.

*Opposite:*

*This collection of silver hollowware includes a George II coffee pot from 1760.*

Before buying antique silver, there are a number of things you should check. Is it pitted or dented? Silver can be costly to repair, and silver plate is more difficult to repair than sterling.

When buying candlesticks, check to see if the mark on both pieces is the same. Breathe hard on the hallmark; if it has been added from another piece you will see the outline.

It is easier to identify English silver than American silver because of the British hallmark system dating back nearly 600 years. After the middle of the 19th century, Americans stamped "sterling" on their pieces, short for Easterling, England.

Monograms, although they might not be your own, are considered by some collectors a lost art form. They do not detract from the value of a piece.

*This silver bowl was designed by Charles Stuart Harris, London, 1896.*

# Tip Trays

At just 6" long, tip trays were the perfect size to hold money. Now they're the perfect size for a collector with little space.

Metal tip trays sprang up in cafes and saloons around the turn of the last century as a way to advertise products. A softly colored pastoral scene of cows grazing decorates one tip tray advertising Carnation dairy products; a view of New York City's Queensboro Bridge advertises Bloomingdale's on another tray.

Some trays picture the item they are advertising, from soaps to sewing machines to chewing gum. Other trays are painted with seemingly unrelated scenes; a woman wearing a bonnet is featured on a tray advertising beer, while horses decorate another tray advertising cigars.

Collections can be built on a theme such as cruise ships or destinations, with the name of a product appearing only on the tray's border.

*These trays advertise safety pins, flat irons, and sewing machines.*

Tip trays were an innovative way to promote a product before television. A customer looked at the tray each time they gave their money to a waiter or collected change in a tavern, restaurant, or ice cream parlor. The more detail in a tip tray, the bigger the price tag.

## Spotting a Fake

The lithographed reproductions flooding the market today look new. They are brighter than vintage trays, which usually are somewhat faded and may show other hints of age, like tiny scratches.

*Left:*

*These round and rectangular trays represent different cities and a Boston newspaper.*

*Opposite:*

*Tip trays were an important accessory and a collectible souvenir for ocean voyages. Cunard Line, Cleveland and Buffalo, and American Line commissioned the design of these trays especially for their companies.*

# Galvanized Watering Cans

With the surge of interest in vintage garden tools, none are more collected or more charming than the hugely popular galvanized metal watering can.

Generally speaking, American cans have shorter spouts and smaller nozzles than their German, French, and English cousins. Some cans are fussy, featuring French tole painting and curvy upturned spouts, while others are unpainted metal for a real farmhouse feel. And there are enough designs floating around to fit every personality. Some cans are short and portly, others tall and regal. There are cans that look like elephants, their trunks serving as the spout, and cans with elegant looping handles.

Back in the 1880s, Britain's John Haws patented a watering can, originally called a watering pail, with perfect balance. Haws disliked the French design with its handle spanning both the back and the top. His design features a handle on the side and a spout with a nose or nozzle. Its balance resembles a teapot.

# paper, plastics & more

.........................................

## chapter four

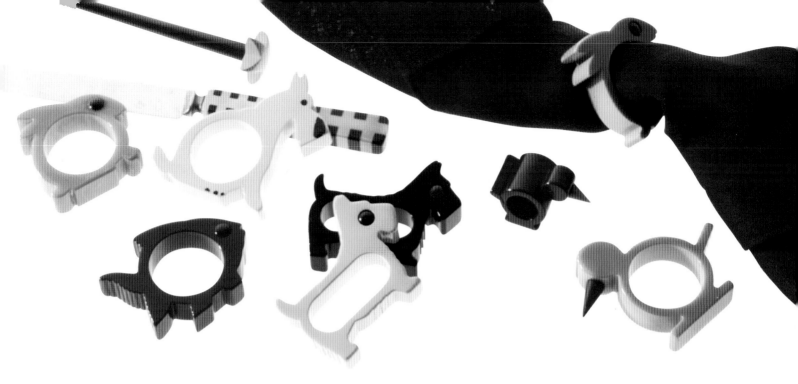

# Bakelite

Bakelite sent a charge through collectors almost as soon as it made its debut in the early 1920s. Nevermind that the material was invented for use in electrical appliances.

Its lightweight and castable qualities proved ideal for making inexpensive bracelets, rings, pins, and other jewelry. Designers seized on the carve-able, etch-able, colorize-able Bakelite as a substitute for pricier materials. No less than Coco Chanel embraced the hard plastic, giving it instant cachet with a line of jewelry and accessories.

Waves of imported reproductions continue to hit the secondary market with faux pieces dubbed Fakelite. The fakes may look good when viewed on a computer screen, but will not stand up to in-hand inspection. Carvings may be crude and colors overly bright.

*Top:*

*Napkin rings shaped like animals or birds are collectors' favorites.*

*Opposite:*

*Bakelite was used to create utensils, jewelry, and buttons.*

Genuine vintage Bakelite has a mellow patina of oxidized colors and an overall aged look, with the years tempering whites into creamy hues.

Bakelite, a phenolic resin plastic created 100 years ago by Belgian chemist Dr. Leo Baekeland, was first used in electrical appliances because of its resistance to heat. Later, its uses expanded to include children's toys, napkin rings, kitchen utensils, jewelry, flatware, poker chips, and place card holders, to name a few.

When the patent for Bakelite ran out in 1927, a similar product with the trade name Catalan came on the market. It quickly became as desirable as Bakelite and often is referred to as Bakelite. It is a durable material, but the occasional chip or crack will lower a piece's value.

*Bakelite flatware is durable, making it practical for use.*

## Spotting a Fake

To identify genuine Bakelite, run the piece under hot water. If it gives off an acid odor, it is probably Bakelite. The imported Fakelite pieces have been treated to mislead collectors by giving off a similar scent. Inspect pieces carefully; a chalky look on a carved area is a sure sign of Fakelite.

# Celluloid

Getting an expensive look for less is something many of us take for granted today. But imagine being a member of the working class at the turn of the last century.

The finer things in life, like jewelry with tortoiseshell, ivory, coral, jet, amber, and other pricey pieces, simply were out of reach. That is, until a plant-based plastic called celluloid leveled the playing field. For the first time, the working class could afford the fashionable look of the wealthy, as celluloid could be made to resemble expensive jewelry pieces.

Most collectors focus on one category, such as celluloid-covered autograph and photograph albums, boxes, or pieces that mimic ivory.

*These boxes each have pastoral scenes on top, set off by floral paper bottoms.*

You might find a glove box with the identification, *Copyright 1885 by L. Prang & Co., Boston,* but signed pieces are rare. Instead, recognizing the work of famous artists of the period will tell you more about your finds. Become familiar with the work of Jean Francis Millet or Hollywood society artist Paul DeLongepre.

Celluloid-preserved artwork of flowers, beautiful women, and children can turn casual lookers into enthusiastic collectors. Lithographs by artists of children's storybooks, including Frances Brundage and Maude Bogart (the mother of Humphrey Bogart), were preserved under a sheet of protective celluloid.

*Top:*

*Celluloid could be made to resemble expensive French ivory. Pictured here is a powder puff set, calendar, vanity tray, and ring box.*

*Opposite:*

*Autograph albums with celluloid covers were popular.*

# Mother-of-Pearl

A protective layer never looked so good as mother-of-pearl. It's hard to resist this iridescent material, which is a secretion of oysters and mollusks that is deposited inside their shells to keep out harmful parasites.

Collectors concentrating on mother-of-pearl (sometimes referred to as organic jewelry) have their choice of thousands of everyday and decorative items to display, study, and swap. The many mother-of-pearl button societies that exist worldwide reflect the fascinating varieties of a humble object made uniquely beautiful.

*Right:*

*The seashell's natural markings simulate a basket weave pattern on these 1940s compacts.*

*Opposite:*

*Treasured for their lovely colors and iridescent luster, mother-of-pearl shells have been used to decorate binoculars, book covers, and boxes. The ink stand at top left would hold two bottles of ink, and a pen would straddle the frame at the back.*

Short on space? Collect smaller objects embellished with mother-of-pearl, such as buttons, hair ornaments, utensils, rings, and pendants. For those with space to spare, it's possible to fill an entire room with furniture featuring mother-of-pearl inlay.

During the Victorian era, flatware with mother-of-pearl handles was a popular wedding present. Furniture with mother-of-pearl inlay was another favorite as were pill boxes, change purses, and gaming tokens such as checker pieces. Today's collector is more apt to focus on jewelry such as cuff links, tie clips, watch faces, or earrings. Knives and pens, either old or new, are also sought after.

## Spotting a Fake

Look at a piece to see if it has the iridescent glow of mother-of-pearl without a distinct pattern or the obvious swirl pattern of plastic; if these markings are evident, you likely have a fake.

*Sets of mother-of-pearl flatware were welcome wedding gifts during the Victorian era.*

# Photographs

Avid collectors of vintage photographs find pleasure in putting a story to the picture, particularly in researching the type of paper on which the photo is printed, how it was printed, special markings and notations, the dress and surroundings of the subject, and other details.

Zero in on a particular theme when collecting photographs. Whatever pulls at your heartstrings likely will give your collection impact and focus. Consider birthday and holiday celebrations, weddings, anniversaries, women in history, outdoorsmen, men in uniform, classic cars, or dogs. You also could gather images evoking an emotion or representing a stage of life, such as childhood innocence.

Look to see what is printed on the back of the photograph. The name of a photographer's studio and the type of paper used should hold clues to the age of the photo. Old cars, household items, clothing, and hairstyles can help date a photograph. Other possible clues: the size of the image and the photographer's imprint, which can lead you to the location and time period the photographer was in business.

*Photographs should be preserved in an archival-quality box.*

# Postcards

Few activities are more delightful for the passionate collector than finding a special treasure while rummaging through boxes of old postcards.

If the postmark is indistinct, the postage stamp will help date a postcard. Album marks, discoloration from acidic paper and ink, and indentations on the corners of a card will lower its value.

Experienced collectors suggest narrowing a collection to what interests you. Collect by town, profession, or hobby. Hot themes are Christmas, Easter, Halloween, and Valentine's Day. Other popular categories for antique postcards include advertising, movie stars, aviation, nudes, signed artist, dogs, fire, African American, and political.

Postcards were invented globally within a few years of one another. John P. Charlton of Philadelphia came out with a postcard in 1861. He later transferred the copyright to his fellow Philadelphian, H. L. Lipman. The Lipman's Postal Card offered a blank front for writing messages. The back was inscribed with three lines—one with a patent mark, the other two for addressing and stamping.

Austria produced the first postcards a few months before the start of the Franco-German War. A German statesman suggested postcards as an advantageous mode of communication for the military. A year later in 1870, the postcard was officially issued in Great Britain with a half-penny stamp printed in the corner.

# Scissor Cuts

The art of the scissor cut is as old as the invention of paper itself, starting as far back as the Han Dynasty in China (206 B.C. to 221 A.D.) and continuing to this day.

A simple pair of scissors or a knife is used to cut intricate and hairline-thin designs, creating paper art reflecting the culture of the region where it was made.

*Scherenschmitte*, which is the German name for scissor cuts, is used extensively throughout Europe, the United States, and Canada. This magical art is called *Papel Picado* in Mexico and *Wyeinki* in rural Poland.

*The Guild of American Papercutters* boasts members from Asia, Europe, Mexico, and Canada, 17 countries in all.

*A black paper cut in a symmetrical pattern is mounted on tan paper and placed in a wooden frame with a striated pattern.*

# Stone Fruit

**M**any pieces of stone fruit are so realistic that it takes a second glance to detect the differences between what Mother Nature made and what man extracted from a quarry.

Stone fruit ripened to collectible status in the early 1900s, with interest peaking somewhat in the 1950s. Stone watermelon slices and nuts present a challenge, but oranges, apples, pears, grapes, and figs are easier to find.

A visit to the town of Volterra, Italy, perched high on a Tuscan mountain, reveals a rich bounty of alabaster stone fruit sold in small shops. Stone fruit has been made by generation after generation of family members. After they're carved by hand, the pieces are painted and then baked to seal their lovely color.

Marble stone fruit is made in the Carrara area of Italy, where the famous quarries Michelangelo used are located. After the marble is carved, it is heated in an oven. The marble pieces are then coated with layers of warm wax mixed with natural pigments and dyes.

## Spotting a Fake

When buying, inspect each piece carefully. You will seldom find cracks, but you will find fruit that is scuffed or chipped, showing dents and dings. Vintage pieces tend to be more finely detailed than copies. The real deal has a muted and dull surface, while new fruit tends to be shiny.

# Theorems

*To create the illusion of age, a contemporary theorem maker has bathed the cotton velveteen with strong coffee. The frame is embellished with false graining.*

Theorem painting is an early American decorative technique that dates back to the first half of the 19th century.

As the name suggests, the cohesive composition is achieved through a series of stencils cut so that no two areas immediately next to each other can be placed on the same stencil. Thus, any theorem will require the sequence of two or more stencils or overlays.

Collectors' personal tastes determine the type of theorems they seek. Some are enchanted by the naive and whimsical, reminiscent of the work of schoolgirls of the early 1800s who made them in abundance. These were usually unsigned stencil paintings on velvet. Other collectors prefer more elegant and sophisticated designs of watercolors on paper or wood. It might be possible to date an antique theorem if it is documented as part of a well-known collection.

Since the resurgence of interest in theorem painting in the 1970s, a number of contemporary artists have emerged. This new work is signed, dated, and sought after by avid collectors. All have perfected their own signature style with baskets, bowls, and flowers—motifs used more frequently than animals, birds, and butterflies. The art form is said to have originated in China hundreds of years ago, spreading to England and then to America.

**Collector's Note: Cletues to the Age**

Antique theorems can be dated by the items depicted in the image. Pressed-glass compotes, for example, were not made before the 1830s.

# Wicker

Old or new, few furnishings have the feeling of summer like wicker.

There is a visual freshness and airy look to woven wicker furniture and accessories that captivated the imagination during its heyday from the mid-1800s until the beginning of the Depression. Some collectors are addicted to antique hand-woven items, while others are satisfied with the machine-made pieces of today.

Wicker has its origins in the Egyptian tradition of basketry, reaching as far back as 4000 B.C. From there, it spread to Greece, China, the Roman Empire, and Medieval England, and wicker continues to hold interest in today's culture. Traditional wicker is hand-woven core, canes, or rattan stalks of a plant. Reed or bamboo is also used. Modern wicker can be woven of plastic. It is amazing to see what restoration artists can do to reclaim pieces that are worn and bent out of shape. With expert workmanship, pieces can become like new.

Keep in mind, though, that poor-quality wicker reproductions mimic the Victorian style.

*Some specialty shops only sell antique wicker furniture like this rocking chair.*

# fashion
# & beauty

···········································

## chapter five

Aurelia M. Buell

# Compacts

Far be it for a proper lady to attend a social function without her compact in hand—or in her handbag.

These pint-sized works of art, some made by famous jewelry houses like Tiffany, Cartier, and Van Cleef & Arpels, were just as elegant as the women who carried them.

By the 1920s, countless companies around the globe were making compacts. Today you can find names like Gwenda British Made, Evans, and Elgin American stamped on the back of the silver-plate or brass base.

Some compacts were decked out in celluloid or enamel flowers, scenes, or destinations, while others were encrusted in jewels or shaped like hearts and other figures. There's even a cigarette and lighter combo compact.

*Right:*

*The flapjack-style compact is thin and named after the pancake.*

*Opposite:*

*Compacts were filled with loose powder or rouge.*

Compacts were made with a wrist chain, finger ring, or a small handle, and filled with loose powder or rouge, making it one of the key accessories of the day.

Collecting vintage compacts will give you the delightful pleasure of rediscovering the fabulous fashions of the past. It is a little piece of the fascinating history of women.

Compacts decorated with jewels were used for dressier occasions.

Collector's Note:
## Cleaning & Storing Compacts

Careful cleaning assures that compacts will maintain their value. Some things to keep in mind:

- By using a soft cloth, compacts can be buffed with a silicone polish.

- Mirrors can be cleaned with a glass cleaner.

- Do not wash a compact by immersing it in water, which can seep behind the mirror and damage the reflective coating.

- Before storing your compacts, be sure to remove all of the powder, the sifter, and the powder puff.

- Wrapping compacts in acid-free tissue paper will help preserve them.

Collector's Note: **Learn the Lingo**

Becoming familiar with the terms relating to compacts is important. *Pressed powder* was the dry face powder used during the 1920s and 1930s. A *sifter box* refers to loose powder. The *cartouche* is the decorative framed space in which initials are engraved.

# Dresser Jars

If you come across a jar with a heavily cut glass bottom and a sterling silver top, you've just discovered the dresser jar.

Dresser jars evoke the splendor and style of a bygone era. Most collectors concentrate on jars ranging from the Victorian age through the 1950s. Sometimes an entire set is available, but more often a single piece of what was once a seven-piece grooming set comes on the market.

You might find *Cranes, Birmingham, England 1924* engraved in the sterling silver lid, or *Cartier, New York 14K* on the inside of a gold lid. The glass bottom could be etched with the manufacturer's name.

Styles and designs vary greatly, making it easy to collect a theme, such as Art Nouveau or Art Deco jars. Some collectors limit their treasure troves to pieces made in England, France, or America.

*Dresser jars held a lady's necessities, from pearls to powder. This clear-cut crystal jar with a sterling silver top is an American piece by Whiting c. 1910–1920.*

Sometimes a famous glass company like Steuben or Hawkes would collaborate with a single maker of silver lids. Cut crystal provides a clue to its age.

Before buying a dresser jar, examine the piece carefully. If it is marked with the maker's name, it will be relatively easy to identify the artist and date the jar. The glass should be without chips or cracks and the lids should not be spotted or pitted.

## Spotting a Fake
..................................................
If the glass has a greasy feel, the dresser jar is probably a reproduction. The mark inside the silver top is the best clue to the age and maker of a jar.

*Left:*

*Those on the tray are enamel-topped American c. 1920; the bottle on its side and the jar behind it were once part of a French lady's traveling set.*

*Opposite:*

*These Art Nouveau sterling silver tops c. 1910–1920 are by Unger & Kerr. Note the monograms on the mirror and the jar at the top left.*

# Hair Combs

Before pixie cuts and bobs, there was the hair comb to pin up a woman's long locks.

For thousands of years, until early in the 20th century, hair combs in every imaginable material and design were an important part of a woman's daily life. Long hair was to be expected. Early combs, made of bone, ivory, wood, brass, silver, or tin, were not only functional but also decorative, reflecting the culture of the time. Later, hand-carved horn, hawksbull turtle, and blush celluloid became the materials of choice and are favored by many collectors.

Vintage combs may be marked *Yai-Go* for a Japanese artist, *C.E. Schutz* for its German designer, or simply *Riviera, Hand Made, Made in France*.

Although no longer a part of a woman's everyday life, dozens of talented craftspeople are still creating new combs. Some feature new designs while others, like the butterfly hair comb seen in the motion picture *Titanic*, represent vintage styles. Reproductions of this comb were authorized for sale by 20th Century Fox and stamped *1998 Fox*.

*Right:*

*Blue teal swirls enhance a pair of Art Deco-style combs.*

*Opposite:*

*Cutwork celluloid combs were made in amber, clear, black, and tortoise. Multi-colored glass inverts sparkled in candlelight.*

If you are lucky, you will find fanciful hair combs at a flea market or estate sale. Many listed on online auction sites are said to have been discovered at estate sales. Be prepared to spend big bucks if you buy at an auction like the one Sotheby's held in Switzerland years ago featuring pieces that once belonged to European royalty.

*Each of these amber combs varies in shape and decoration.*

# Hats

Time was when neither man nor woman left the house without wearing a hat. Protective coverings for the head have been important since pre-historic ages, but hats with style that are fashion statements have been in vogue for a couple hundred years.

Collectors are most likely to concentrate on an era or the creation of a particular designer. The *Gibson Girl* look, large hats embellished with feathers, birds, and flowers and accents of tulle and lace, may appeal to you. Alternatively, you might go for a Cartwright style with yards and yards of lace over a wire frame. Christian Dior is credited with introducing the small, narrow pillbox hats popular in the 1940s and '50s. These tiny artistic endeavors are more of an ornament for the head than a protection from the sun.

Many hats are labeled with the name of the designer, the store where they are sold, and their size. A label could read *Anne Fogarty of Saks Fifth Avenue* or *Lazarus Model, Cincinnati, Paris*. There are prominent emerging milliners such as Marie Galvin. Look online to feast upon her imaginative styles and use of materials.

# Lockets

Antique lockets are testaments to loves of long ago. A locket might hold a lock of hair or a photograph of a beloved one, along with engraved initials or symbols with a special meaning. A.E.I. stood for *Amenity, Eternity, Infinity*, while I.M.O. meant *In Memory Of*. An ivy leaf engraved on a locket represents eternity.

English, French, and German hallmarks, in addition to the maker's initials or marks, help date and identify lockets. American lockets might be engraved with the manufacturer's name, such as Bliss Brothers or W. S. Blankliton, both Massachusetts companies. The French export hallmark is a Mercury head of 18K.

*Above:*

*Eight late-Victorian gold lockets make a fascinating bracelet.*

*Opposite:*

*All of these small treasures open to reveal compartments for photographs or locks of hair.*

Celebrity lockets containing photographs of famous people, like Edward VII and Alexandria of England, or Otto Von Bismark and Kaiser Frederick III of Germany, could be a collector's area of concentration. Another collector might specialize in men's, religious, or Celtic lockets, or perhaps heart-shaped pieces engraved with "I Love You."

Some are attracted to a design period like Art Nouveau or Art Deco. Japanese designs on lockets are another of the countless possibilities for a theme, to narrow the search and add excitement to the hunt.

*The bow pin at the neck holds a diamond and black enamel heart-shaped locket, c. 1875, France. Below is a c. 1880 black enamel oval with gold and diamonds that also originated in France. The onyx locket, upper left, hangs on a bow-shaped pin.*

### Collector's Note: **Get Real**
· · · · · · · · · · · · · · · · · · · · · · · · · · · · · · · · · · · ·
Whether starting a collection or adding to one, look for lockets with original glass, not plastic, in the interior bezel of a piece.

# Perfume Bottles

Until early in the 20th century, perfume was purchased in plain containers and transferred to decorative bottles.

Collectors of perfume bottles usually specialize in one of the two broad categories: commercial, with the bottle and its contents being marketed and sold together, or non-commercial, with the bottle as a separate entity. The latter had been exclusive until 1907, when the French glass designer Rene Lalique created lovely glass bottles especially for Coty perfumes. The new concept exploded with perfumes in their own beautiful bottles sold over the counter by the thousands.

Few makers of early perfume bottles are known, but they illustrate the prevailing design of the period in an amazing array of shapes and materials. Glass perfume bottles from Roman times in a deep rich blue or honey color have been excavated. English clear-cut crystal with silver trim, Russian cloisonné, and Eastern European Bohemian glass are 19th-century treasures.

*The smaller bottle is commercial, with some of the original perfume still inside. The original atomizer is missing from the tall bottle.*

The double-ended bottle with embossed silver caps at both ends peaked during Victorian days. Bottles with a pop-up atomizer pump appeared late in the 19th century. Rubber ball atomizers came into their own in the early 20th century. The ever-present glass stopper usually repeats the design of the bottle itself.

Collector's Note:
**Timeless in a Bottle**
............................................
The classic design for the Chanel No. 5 bottle has remained virtually unchanged since 1922, when it was first introduced by Coco Chanel.

*Left:*

*Original atomizers survived on two of these DeVilbiss perfume bottles from the early 1900s. Crocheted silk covers the rubber atomizer bulbs.*

*Opposite:*
*Czechoslovakian perfume bottles such as these can be found with their labels intact.*

# Shoes

If you feel a tinge of excitement when you spot the smart style of a stiletto heal, collecting vintage shoes of the 1950s and '60s might be for you. Shoe styles reflect the constantly shifting perspectives and passions of the era in which they were designed.

Vintage shoes are those from another era with an aesthetic quality that makes them stand out. The crystal-encrusted red stilettos that brought 7,000 pounds at a charity auction in England are representative of the explosion in color, texture, shape, and style that dominated shoe design throughout the 20th century.

Protective leather boots, characteristic of the 19th century, gave way to the varied uses of materials and endless imaginative designs that followed. Prominent designer Patrick Cox produces limited editions especially for collectors.

Collectors seek the work of top designers, with Vivienne Westwood ranking high on the list. You may be drawn to slingbacks by Yves Saint Laurent or the innovative plastic creations of Mary Quant. Roger Vivier is considered a shoemaking hero. Today's designers are said to frequent vintage clothing stores for inspiration.

# Vintage Purses

Most women agree, you can never have too many handbags.

One of the wonderful things about vintage purses is that they can be worn as an instant fashion statement and also displayed, grouped as a collection. In various styles to suit the needs of an era, they have been around for hundreds of years.

Some consider the beaded bag to be the most collectible and treasured. They are fragile and appreciated for the many hours that went into making them by hand.

The mesh bag was especially popular during the late 1800s but only became affordable after a mesh machine was patented and put into use in 1908. They then became the hottest thing on the market. Whiting & Davis became synonymous with top-of-the-line mesh bags.

Italian designer Elsa Schiaparelli and French designer Ann Marie were important, not only for their own work but for their influence on handbag design for the years that followed. Ann Marie's themed bags of the 1930s, like the *Music* collection, which played tunes when opened, attracted attention. Savvy collectors seek the French designer's piano, clock, and telephone bags, to mention a few.

Collector's Note: **Purchase Pointers**
. . . . . . . . . . . . . . . . . . . . . . . . . . . . . . . . . . .
While on the hunt for vintage purses, keep in mind that all designer handbags are signed. Also, a silk lining that has been replaced does not diminish the value. However, if there is a strong chemical odor inside a 1950s Lucite bag, do not buy it as the plastic is deteriorating.

*Left:*

*All four of these vintage bags have metal closures.*

*Opposite:*

*Collectors agree vintage purses are romantic, adding an accent to any outfit. They were made in a surprising variety of designs, sizes, shapes, and colors.*

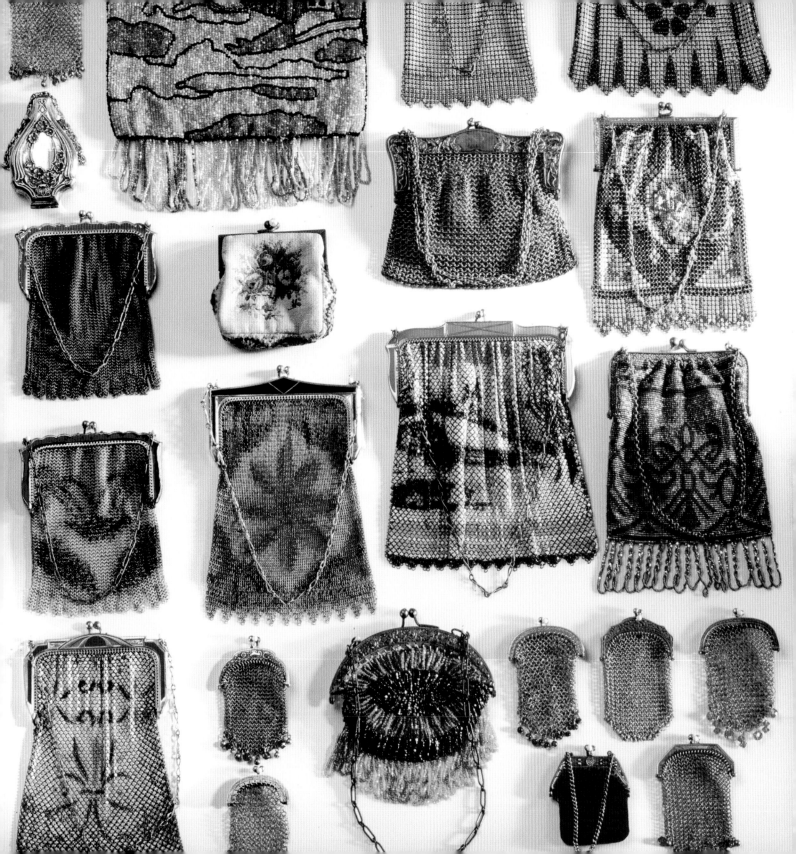

# Suffragette Jewelry

While chains and locks may be common on today's jewelry, these elements on bracelets and pins once symbolized oppression.

The dedicated struggle for women's emancipation during the Edwardian and Art Nouveau eras inspired suffragette jewelry. More suffragette jewelry was made in England than in the United States.

The colors of the movement—*purple* for royalty and the instinct for freedom and dignity, *white* for purity in both public and private life, and *green* for hope and the emblem of spring—dominate the decoration of necklaces, pins, brooches, and bracelets. Wearing jewelry in these colors was an announcement of one's allegiance to the cause. Stones from Bohemia were exported to England to decorate these pieces.

*Right:*

*Gold bar pins and padlocks are typical of the pieces made in the United States.*

*Opposite:*

*Suffragette jewelry for wealthy women included pins, necklaces, and brooches decorated with stones in the symbolic white, green, and purple. This group spans 1908–1918.*

W & F. TEESY
JEWELLERS
8, VICTORIA ST
& 70, STRETFORD RD
MANCHESTER

It takes careful examination of hinge styles to date a piece. Familiarity with the types of screws used will allow one to separate vintage from a reproduction. In addition to jewelry, badges and flags of some of the suffragette organizations are being copied today.

Even though most reproductions are advertised as such, it is wise for a novice collector to work with a knowledgeable and reputable dealer.

Collector's Note:
**United They Stood**
. . . . . . . . . . . . . . . . . . . . . . . . . . . . .
Men supported the cause by wearing cufflinks, rings, and tie tacks with the trumpet-for-freedom design or the symbolic colors of the movement.

*Working lock clasps were reminders of the hardship, subjugation, and oppression women faced during the era. The set in the blue box was made in England.*

# Sunglasses

One of the best things about collecting vintage sunglasses is that they never go out of style.

The retro look is always in fashion; it all depends on your personal preferences. You can collect by designer like Gucci, as the ultimate in sophistication; Chanel for classic design; or Germany's Eschenbach, known for his aviator style. The work of the innovative Italian designer Alain Mikli or France's Emmanuelle Khanh is also worth serious consideration. Most of the names associated with sunglasses are well known in the fashion industry, including Cartier, LaCroix, LaCoste, Dior, and Cardin.

Sunglasses began less as a fashion statement than as a ruse. It all started in 15th-century China, when judges wore sunglasses to hide their expressions during a trial. Today's celebrities probably feel more private behind these fashion accessories as well.

*Black-and-white plastic twists protruding from the top of this frame are a whimsical favorite.*

Years ago, *Ad Age* named the Foster Grant Company's campaign, *Who's Behind Those Foster Grants* featuring a host of celebrities like Woody Allen, Sophia Loren, and Raquel Welch, as one of the all-time hundred best advertisements.

The new Oakley sunglasses with a built-in digital audio player received excellent reviews. These are considered collectible even though new. Vintage eyeware from the 1950s on is affordable and quite easy to locate.

## Spotting a Fake

If you can scratch off the designer's name or logo, or the hinges do not have the look of quality, the pair of sunglasses is probably a fake.

*Left:*

*Frames were frequently selected first and lenses added later.*

*Opposite:*

*Frames with side shields, such as those at the upper right and upper left, are suitable to wear at the beach. The Italian company Persol, known for its side shields, manufactured the pair at the upper left.*

# folk art

....................

## chapter six

# Baskets

Fashioned from willow, pine needles, oak, and sea grass, every culture since the beginning of time has made use of the basket.

Simple or complex patterns, determined by the weaving technique and the type of material used, could be strictly decorative or intended to define a specific use for each basket.

Basket design is limited only by the maker's imagination. Indians made tightly woven baskets to gather and store grains. Some of these weaves were so tight that they could actually hold water, and were even used for cooking. Large open-weave Shaker baskets lined with cheese cloth were used to separate curds from whey in the cheese-making process. The Japanese created lovely ikebana baskets of woven bamboo. Older baskets like these are very rare and expensive.

Simple willow baskets, used as picnic hampers or for gathering fruit, are easier to find and much less costly for the beginning collector. Also plentiful are ribbed baskets with fixed handles. Some like the *butt* or *fanny* basket, named for its two-cheek appearance, which was used primarily for eggs.

*Displayed as a collage, a basket collection adds sculptural charm to country decorating.*

# Belsnickels

While their expressions are anything but jolly,
Belsnickels haven't scared off collectors.

Called the *Curmudgeons of Christmas*, legend has it
that these angry-looking figures would come, tree
branch switch in hand, seeking out naughty children.

Nineteenth-century German folklore tells of Pelsnickel
(Furry Nicholas), a character covered from head to
toe in fur who roamed the countryside, announc-
ing his arrival by banging his switch on doors
and windows.

The Santa Claus we know today is in
part descended from the mythical gift
giver who would cull the naughty
from the nice, bestowing small
trinkets on the nice and corporal
punishment on the naughty. A
child might be granted reprieve
from punishment if they sang a
song or recited a poem that
amused the Belsnickel.

*This trio of fragile antique
Belsnickels is protected by a
glass dome. It is unusual to find a
trio each with a different color coat.*

Early Belsnickels from the 1870s to 1900 held real goose feather trees and were made of papier-mâché. If you can find them now, the figures command high prices. Even the old solid chalkware figures made by the Pennsylvania Germans are expensive.

*Left:*

*A Belsnickel with the traditional tree branch switch wears a red coat with snow trim more often associated with his happier cousin, Santa.*

*Below:*

*A Belsnickel with his tree branch switch has been wandering the country-side before arriving with a sleigh full of toys for good children.*

Collector's Note:

**Sour Faces versus Smiles**

If an old-fashioned Christmas figure is smiling he is a Santa rather than a Belsnickel, which are known for their sour expressions.

*Opposite:*

*Both antique and new Belsnickels, like this one in a sleigh, are frequently covered with glittering mica and tiny snowflakes.*

# Bottle Cap Sculpture

Bottle cap sculpture, long considered a poor relative of established folk art, has achieved recognition in both anonymous pieces and those of named artists on display in dozens of museums around the world.

Its beginnings are somewhat obscure and baffling. Some credit a magazine article in the 1940s with initiating the idea. Others call attention to the fact that Clarence and Grace Woolsey, who some dealers claim are the most significant folk artists discovered during the 1990s, began making fanciful pieces as early as 1961.

Shows today might feature bottle cap sculptures from Nigeria, South Africa, Australia, and the United States, to name a few. A 6' bottle cap giraffe on a skateboard is one of the most popular permanent exhibits at the Smithsonian. It is included in must-see lists for visitors to Washington, D.C. These anonymous figures, so abundant on thrift shop shelves during the 1980s, leaped into antique shops and from there into art galleries. Galleries often feature the work of a single emerging bottle cap artist.

*The collector of this bottle cap sculpture by artist Clarence Woolsey has named this piece Martian Man.*

# Chalkware

Ceramic figures made in factories share their shelf in history with the countless homemade versions.

Made for fun by common people, vintage chalkware is pure folk art. It required considerable skill, but no formal training. Many of the pieces have identical size and form, usually two halves that have been glued together. Some makers attempted to copy more expensive versions such as Staffordshire, but more often the creations were simple with a sense of whimsy.

The watercolor or oil-painted decorations gave pieces their uniqueness. Frequently, apples were painted purple or blue. This was not unlike the work of the Italians, who carried

well-worn molds from their native country, decorating their wares in vivid colors.

Since 19th-century chalkware is rare and expensive, some collectors concentrate on carnival chalk, which was made well into the 20th century. These pieces manufactured as carnival prizes can be found in the shape of a kewpie doll or politically incorrect ethnic figure. Much carnival chalkware is dated on the rim of its base.

Twentieth-century carnival chalk is a far cry from the 19th-century nodders, which are chalkware figures with bobbing heads, composed of two separately poured pieces and joined by hooks inserted in the plaster.

# Decoys

Countless decoys crudely honed or delicately carved lure more than the unsuspecting fowl. Usually at a distance from a hidden duck in a swampy lake, decoys attract not only bird hunters but also collectors who would never think of picking up a gun.

More than 2,000 years ago decoys were fashioned from cattail bulrush, tule plant, and tamarack sticks. Sometimes the sticks or reeds were covered with duck skins. Writings from 1678 describe coy decoys as coming from the Dutch word *de kooj*, meaning to trap.

Most collectors focus their interests on wood-carved decoys, usually basswood or sugar pine. When beginning a collection, choose an area of concentration. You may want decoys used in the area where you hunt or you may focus on a style or the work of one carver.

As with almost any collectible, condition is everything. Is the paint original? Look for areas where the paint may be shiny and others where it is dull. This is a clue to a touch-up.

Use a magnifying glass or even black light to check the paint. Another common problem is a decoy head that is not original to the body. Documentation as to the decoy's history is valuable.

*Top:*

*These decoys have various origins. The pair of Mallard ducks is labeled Mason Animal Trap Company. The two ducks have the initials A.F. incised. The remaining are unlabeled.*

*Opposite:*

*The shoreline bird carvings are by Elmer Crowell. The smaller carving on the left represents a Jack Snipe; the larger bird is a carving of a winter yellowbird.*

# Fishing Lures

There are, it seems, as many different lures to be collected as there are fish in the sea.

Manufactured all over the world, with some companies, such as Swift International, advertising 10,000 lures in stock, collectors often join clubs related to their particular interest. Fishing holidays attract sportsmen to Finland, New Zealand, and many other places.

*Above:*

*Lures with wooden or glass eyes in good condition, such as the one in the second section from the top, are very collectible.*

Among the thousands of types to collect one might like the Green Wing Teal, with green tips on the wings and a green patch on the face; the Greenhead Pintail Drake, with its yellow beak, green head, and white stripe around the neck; or the Mallard Drake Ice Duck with a black stripe down its back.

Narrowing your collection to the lures of one company, period, location, or type of fish is a good idea. Before starting to buy, learn as much as you can about your particular area of interest. There are countless books with helpful hints and instructions on how to start a collection. Also, talk to other lure collectors at tackle shows.

By reading and looking at enough lures you will learn how to evaluate condition. Because the making of lures is so vast and varied, the collector has the thrill of occasionally coming upon some he has never seen before.

Collector's Note: **Vying for Value**

The most sought-after collectibles are the hand-painted lures with glass eyes, produced from 1900 to 1941. Lure condition is determined on a scale of 1 to 10, with 10 being NIB (New in Box), meaning unused and placed in the original box or carton.

# Miniature Sheep

There wasn't a child in Germany who didn't pine after these adorable miniature sheep, sold by street vendors at the turn of the last century.

Called stick leg sheep or German wooly sheep, miniature sheep are usually 2"–4" tall. They originated in the Erzgebirge toy-making area in what was once East Germany. If you are lucky enough you might find one in its original box, either cardboard or wood. It might be marked *German Erzgebirge Seiffen*, or you might find *Germany* inside one leg, or stamped on the paper neck band.

A sheep with a red, green, blue, or yellow paper band and working brass bell intact is a real find. Also, check to see if the tiny stick figure will still stand. Some are advertised as having a loose or broken leg. As the faces were hand painted, their expressions differ from sheep to sheep.

Once in a while one comes on the market with wax drippings in its coat. That indicates it was once part of a putz scene under a Christmas tree. The word putz is from the German word putzen, which means to decorate.

Children loved the toy figures so much that they were sold year-round. The vast majority are white, but as in any family, the occasional black sheep can be found. When toy making boomed in Japan after World War II, these tiny creatures were made in that country.

# Native American Folk Art

Many collectors of Native American folk art focus on a type of work or a particular region, or they collect by artist.

Consider the work of a single artist, like the renowned Navajo potter, Wallace Nez, Jr., whose work is owned by collectors and displayed in museums worldwide.

Prolific would be an understatement when describing the spectrum of work created by Native Americans. First, look at baskets, pottery, textiles, jewelry, blankets, rugs, masks, and other treasures that have been produced, and are still being produced, by tribes all over North America. Each offers a variety of styles. You might limit your collection of baskets, for example, to the work of a certain tribe or from one area.

Thousands of books are available, giving tribal histories and background on the art most associated with them. If you are drawn to jewelry, you could limit yourself to metalwork alone, or metal with stones or beads.

# Noah's Arks

In the 19th century, the world cried for more toys and the woodworkers of Germany responded.

In Europe and America, Noah's Arks, made in the Erzgebirge mountain region, were in just about every affluent home. The Victorian sensibility dictated that on the Sabbath children play only with toys having religious themes, which increased the ark's popularity.

In true cottage industry fashion, the making of arks was a family affair. Even the youngest child in a family participated. Some families made the entire art vignette while others may have made only one species of animal to add to a set.

Most arks are not signed and because they were made in a home or multiple homes, the maker is impossible to identify. Some villages created more intricately hand-carved animals and arks painted with more detail.

*The ark on top of the cabinet is c. 1880. It was also made with a yellow-painted exterior. It is not as rare as the c. 1860 ark in the cabinet, which is distinguished by a remarkable hand-painted frieze spanning the front just below the roof.*

Paint with a shiny finish denotes the work of one village while a dull, chalky finish tells the collector that the piece was made in an area other than Erzgebirge. Animals with a shiny paint are more detailed and of higher quality. Animals from another toy-making center, Elastolin, are composition rather than wood.

Most older arks require some sort of professional restoration because of wood deterioration. Pairs of animals in different stances from each other are scarce.

*This c. 1900 ark with two levels of gates has typical Stiffen ring-turned animals. Animal shapes were mass-produced by securing a piece of wood on a lathe to create the shape and then cutting the result into many pieces to become individual animals. Stiffen is one of the best-known villages in the Erzgebirge.*

# Puppets

Some of the first actors to hit the stage, puppets from all over the world are taking center stage once again.

Defined as a figure whose movements are controlled by someone with strings, rods, or hand movements, archaeologists have unearthed puppet-like figures dating as far back as the ancient civilizations of Egypt, Greece, Rome, and the Orient.

In most countries, roaming minstrels performed impromptu roadside shows for the different villages. The shows grew in popularity and as they did, the presentations became more formal.

The name marionette means *little Mary*, and one theory is that the name was derived from the Virgin Mary as the shows were used to teach religion during the 1500s in Europe.

*Puppets made in Myanmar (Burma) have carved wooden heads and elaborate silk clothing.*

# Safety Pin Baskets

A kitschy collectible and a great conversation piece, safety pin baskets from the 1950s and 1960s are colorful finds.

Brightly colored acrylic beads were assembled into baskets, usually with a handle, using the common safety pin and some floral wire to hold them together. Since they were a home craft, the variety of bead combinations and shape differences defies imagination.

Brass and stainless steel worked best, as spring steel has a high iron content and is subject to rusting. The variety of beads, such as red beads shaped like a raspberry or clear faceted beads, gives the baskets their personality. Most were 8"–10" tall, but you will find 3"–4" minis and an occasional giant of a foot or more.

Before buying a safety pin basket, examine it for rust, which will eventually discolor the beads.

*These collectible safety pin baskets are pre-1960.*

# Shaker Boxes

While reproductions have flooded the market worldwide, there are plenty of authentic Shaker boxes still out there.

The Shaker movement had its roots with the French Calvinists, who flourished in southern France in the 17th century, fled to England in the 18th century, and moved on to the United States in the late 1700s.

Known for their clean, graceful lines, these boxes are just one of the Shakers' many designs originally used to store dry goods. Both the Danish and the Japanese have taken to using the small "s" when referring to their shaker boxes. Both early Japanese boxes and the Shaker-made ones in America exhibit a visual lightness and delicate construction.

Historically, before the mid-1800s, Shaker boxes had clear finishes and painted boxes prevailed after that. Small boxes are more rare and command higher prices than larger versions. Many contemporary box makers are using a zero-to-eight numbering system for size, with zero representing the smallest.

*Above:*
*Colors date these boxes as pre-1850.*

*Opposite:*
*Antique Shaker boxes were made in a variety of sizes.*

# Wood Carvings

Name a figure and it most certainly exists in a wood carving. Fish, fowl, flowers, fruit, and, of course, the human form have been shaped from blocks of walnut, basswood, and teak since the beginning of man. Everything imaginable from aardvarks to zebras, no matter what your interest, a talented wood carver has fashioned an amazing likeness of it.

As an art form, woodworking spans the globe. Asia, Africa, Europe, the Americas, and Australia all have rich histories filled with superb examples of wood artistry.

You could hunt for carvings as large as an antique French carousel horse or as heavily carved as an English gargoyle.

*Seasons are celebrated with groups of figurines, such as this collection for fall.*

Perhaps miniature carvings of animals, houses, or human figures pique your interest. Maybe it's mythical or historical figures or even a choir of angels you want to decorate your domicile. You can collect hand-painted carvings or plain varnished wooden ones. Today, contemporary folk artists are producing extraordinary wood carvings with all the attention to detail of the early artists.

*Above:*

*Wooden hens, chicks, and roosters proudly strut their stuff for collectors.*

*Below:*

*Love to fish or just plain love fish? Carvers love them too. You could assemble your own school in no time.*

### Collector's Note: **Making Copies**

Remarkable resin copies are being produced in China with the permission of the carver of the original. Make sure to distinguish between the original wood carving and its resin copy. Expect to pay a lot more for the original.

# textiles

····································

## chapter seven

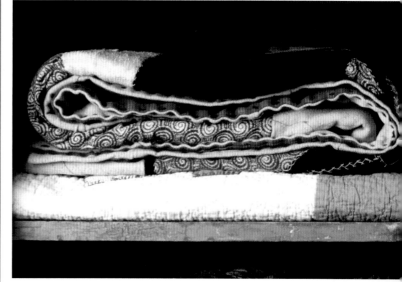

# Coverlets

Practical as well as pretty, coverlets were put to good use, which means they can be hard to find in stellar condition.

Woven wool coverlets kept 18th-century beds cozy and added a splash of color to what was often the most prominent furnishings in the home.

The earliest examples, made by home weavers, featured thick, loosely woven overshot patterns or simple geometric designs. Special loom attachments allowed the weaver to create elaborate designs that incorporated motifs such as buildings, trees, birds, and flowers. Interesting color compositions and complex motifs can boost value, as can historical significance.

In many cases these coverlets have a corner block with the name of the weaver and the client, as well as the location where it was made and the date, which reveals part of the item's past.

*Top:*

*This c. 1820 quilt has a jacquard double-woven Boston town border.*

*Right:*

*With its uncommon jacquard pattern with unevenly spun thread, this quilt was probably from an early factory or perhaps homespun c. 1840.*

*Opposite:*

*This overshot weave c. 1825 coverlet in red, blue, and a rare black is used as a table covering in a historic home.*

# Homespun

When they called it handmade, women from long, long ago certainly meant it.

What we take for granted—everyday fabrics and textiles—were made from scratch several hundred years ago. Rural women spun natural fibers such as cotton, wool, and flax by hand, creating yarns and woven materials for everyday household linens.

This process created sturdy, simple cloth that's come to be known as homespun. And lucky for us, many of these pieces still exist today.

The natural brown and white cotton color of cloth is often accented with stripes, checks, or bands of color created with natural vegetable and plant dyes. These utilitarian textiles, with their soft colors and interesting textures, lend an authentic country touch to any home.

*Top:*

*These blankets were colored with commercial and vegetable dyes.*

*Opposite:*

*These homespun linens are made in the three typical colors—indigo, natural, and tan.*

You are more likely to find homespun items such as blankets and table runners than clothing, which was often patched and worn until it fell apart. In some cases, the fibers from worn-out clothing were repurposed to make new linens.

Collector's Note: **Taking Care**

Some things to keep in mind when caring for your homespun treasures:

- Avoid direct contact with raw wood surfaces; this can cause items to become discolored.

- Line shelves and drawers with clean white cotton sheeting or acid-free tissue. If you are stacking linens, place heavier pieces on the bottom and lighter pieces on top.

- Pad the folds and creases to prevent fabrics from wearing in these areas.

- Clean linens before storage to prevent pest damage. For the first-time washing of any homespun, separate 10–15 yards and use a commercial washer that will handle at least 50 pounds. Wash two to three times using any detergent, hot water, and a liquid softener. In between each washing, untwist the fabric and put it back in the washer.

- Check stored linens regularly for air circulation, moisture, pests, and other changes.

*These fabrics were woven from brown cotton and colored with natural dyes.*

# Hooked Rugs

Early American homemakers recycled nearly any bit of leftover cloth into useful, and often beautiful, new items including hooked rugs.

Using a rug hook, they pulled loops of wool yarn or narrow rag strips through a coarse backing fabric to create personalized floor coverings featuring flowers, animals, geometrics, and other hand-drawn designs. Early backing fabrics were jute, burlap, and even old feed sacks.

Though the earliest rugs were individually designed, by the 1870s many rug hookers began using printed patterns. Though it may be difficult to find antique hooked rugs in good condition, the technique is easy to learn.

Floral designs are fairly common, while people and landscapes are harder to come by. When checking for condition, make sure the backing is intact; this can be difficult to fix. You may be able to repair other damages, such as tears, by using like materials.

# Linens

There's something about crisp, white linens that turns an everyday browser into a devoted collector. Perhaps it's because linens capture the romantic aura of the past; they speak of the promise of a painstakingly prepared trousseau, the gracious afternoon tea party, or the gentility of Victorian pastimes. Or maybe it's because well-preserved linens, laces, and needlework can still be used and displayed today.

Whatever the reason, there's always room in our cupboards for just one more tablecloth, runner, or set of napkins.

When collecting, look for items made with a certain technique, such as embroidery, bobbin lace, or appliqué, or a certain type such as tea towels, handkerchiefs, or pillowcases. Appliqué lace features separate pieces sewn onto fabric; Battenburg, all the rage a century ago, is made by sewing a special lace tape onto a backing and stitching in between; and Chantilly lace is a delicate bobbin lace using silk and linen thread on a hexagonal mesh background to create outlined floral motifs.

*Above:*

*Netting-type lace with fringed edges was popular on bedspreads.*

*Opposite:*

*Pictured are examples of whitework tea cozies and other linens, including cutwork and crochet.*

# Penny Rugs

Penny rugs take their name from the coins used as templates to make the felted wool circles that form their appliqué designs.

Pennies, which were substantially larger in the 1800s, were traced on felted wool to draw perfect circles. These circles were then used to form the appliqué designs of these rugs.

Penny rug makers stitched smaller felt circles to the top of larger ones to form target-like pieces. The colorful folk art mats, which originated in the mid-1800s, were never found underfoot; they were originally designed as table toppers or wall hangings.

Some feature a center design framed by "pennies" and a tongue-shaped border. Authentic penny rugs are rare, but new examples of the art can be found in retail stores, at folk art shows, and online.

**Collector's Note: Off the Floor**

Penny rugs are not rugs at all. They are decorative coverings for tables, beds, and mantels as well as wall hangings.

# Quilts

Quilts have a special way of bringing warmth into a home.

Every piece, whether made in the 19th century or today, contains a unique blend of artistry and emotion. Quilts are hung on walls, set on tables, and laid on beds. From the living room couch to a picnic outdoors, there are few places a quilt won't go.

The three most common types of quilts are pieced, appliqué, and whole cloth. Within these types there are endless variations, and some quilts feature a combination of techniques. In addition to using decorative stitching to secure layers together, a quilt top can be embellished in many ways from painting to embroidery.

If a quilt looks too symmetrical and mechanical, it was likely made from a kit. Kits, which became available around 1935, came with pre-cut fabrics and patterns. While pattern and condition can hint at age, determining the period of the fabric used is the best way to date a quilt. There are several good fabric-dating guides available. These guidebooks include descriptions, full-color photos, and sometimes swatches of fabrics from different eras.

*Above:*

*Pictured are pre-1935 Amish quilts known for their geometric patterns and bold color combinations.*

*Right:*

*This cupboard is stocked with old patchwork and appliqué quilts including several crazy quilts.*

# Samplers

Long before video games and television, there was needle and thread.

Starting in the 18th century, young girls were trying out their stitching skills on small pieces of fabric no larger than a yard square. These earnest efforts are known today as antique samplers.

The name of the maker and the date are usually part of the design. In addition to simple lettering, mottoes, and family history, some of the work contains the maker's personal musings.

Design and condition have the biggest influence on value, even before age. A sampler in its original frame is a valuable find. Though these early samplers are prized, later examples can be just as collectible, including the stamped and stitched versed samplers that arrived on the scene in the 1920s. Even those made today via patterns or kits and reproductions have found a spot on collectors' walls.

*New samplers retain the hand-crafted appeal of their 18th- and 19th-century forebears.*

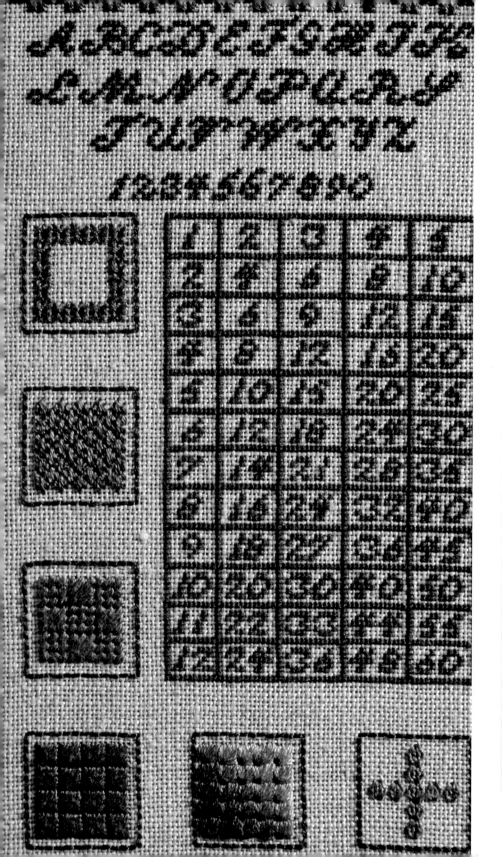

Collector's Note:
**Hanging Your Prize**

. . . . . . . . . . . . . . . . . . . . . . . . . . .

Mount samplers on a padded acid-free mounting board and use a frame made with inert materials that will not discolor the fabric over time. Samplers should be under glass for protection, but the fabric should not touch the glass. If you have a fragile or large sampler, do not try to frame it yourself; ask a skilled professional for help.

Display your samplers with care. Never hang them in direct sunlight or illuminate with spotlights. Do not hang them above a heat source or on outside walls that may be subject to condensation.

# toys

chapter eight

# Metal Toys

It wasn't until late in the 18th century that toy makers looked at metal as a viable material.

Once they got their minds and metals working, toys were soon churned out using cast iron, tinplate, sheet steel, and lead. The use of tinplate (thin sheets of steel covered with tin) began in the late 18th century, and cast iron and sheet steel toys were made in the late 19th century until World War II. Buddy L trucks, for example, were made of pressed sheet steel primarily in the 1920s and '30s, while lead was used principally for making model soldiers.

Japan was the tin toy-producing center of the world, outdistancing Germany after World War I. Although the list of Japanese toy-making companies is extensive, the two companies that had their roots in Japan shortly after World War I that survived are Masudaya and Marusan Co., Ltd. The letters T and M in a diamond is the trademark for the former, while the letters SAN in a circle is the trademark for the latter.

Experienced collectors usually specialize. Some limit themselves to a material such as cast iron or tin, while others chose a theme such as trains, cars, or spring-powered toys. Many antique tin toys were given a thin coat of paint and then stenciled. Cars from the 1930s with working headlights are a collector's choice.

# Nesting Apples

Before nesting dolls, the wooden figures in increasing size that fit inside each other, there was nesting fruit.

Nesting apples were first made in the Russian handicraft center of Semionovo by Arsenty Mayorov, known for his distinctive Russian nesting dolls. The idea for the nesting doll had come to Russia as souvenir dolls from Japan in 1890. Thirty-three countries imported the "just for fun" toys made by the artisans at Semionovo, which was surrounded by dense forests with soil unfit for agriculture.

Some sets contained several apples with the smallest being solid wood. More sought-after sets have a game inside, which looks like a

horse race. Each child playing the game would select a "horse," a round disk with a number on it. They would take turns spinning the wheel until the ball would settle on a number. The child whose number settled on the wheel could move one step forward. The first player to cross the finish line was the winner.

Those playing with their nesting apples should be careful not to damage this nostalgic toy. Its aniline dyes and light touch brush marks could wear off. Condition is paramount to its value.

*Some apples in this group are nests of apples, one inside the other, while others conceal tiny games.*

# Building Blocks

Designed to unleash a child's imagination, building blocks were a staple in many homes.

The advent of less-expensive color lithography during the mid-19th century is credited with the mass production of picture blocks. With a different scene glued to each of the six sides, picture blocks were among the most popular learning toys.

Some collectors concentrate on ABC blocks with a letter accompanied by a corresponding picture beginning with that letter. Although seldom marked, more lithographed blocks were made in Germany than anywhere else.

*The second set of building blocks from the left on the bottom shelf is marked with the initials J.H.S. for the J.H. Singer Company, New York.*

# Children's Sleds

M emories of childhood winters or an old sled in the attic might lead to a collection of these snow-propelled vehicles.

Some children's sleds were made by hand, and many were fashioned and painted in small shops across the snow belts of the world, especially Germany, Switzerland, and the United States.

Most early sleds are non-steerable. The Ram's Head German sled has round runners at the front. A Swiss-made Davos was often built of hickory with bentwood runners. The runners were steam-bent and sometimes covered with iron or steel. American sleds could be built of pine, white ash, or hardwoods. Local woods were most frequently used.

*The date 1906 is stamped on the bottom of this seat.*

*Swan's-head ironwork is loved by collectors.*

Collector's Note:
## Sized for the Sexes
Girls' sleds were usually 10"–12" high. Boys' sleds, called cutters, were 6" off the ground for belly flopping, the age-old practice of running with your sled and flopping down on it as it starts to go down the hill.

# Game Boards

You'd have to go back several centuries to trace the first known game board.

Antique handmade checkerboard and Parcheesi boards date back to the 19th century. The game of checkers dates back to the 16th century, while Parcheesi is rooted in the 4th century in India.

Collectors find an amazing variety of vintage checkers, Parcheesi, and backgammon boards on the market. Some are double-sided with Parcheesi on one side and checkers on the other.

These three most plentiful game boards are followed by carom and crokinole boards, Chinese checkers, chess, and bagatelle, which developed into today's pinball machines.

Game boards were made with several combinations of paint colors. Red, green, yellow, and blue may dominate one board, while another might display the more unusual combination of orange squares on a black background.

*The Parcheesi board with its bright colors is nearly 100 years old. The checkerboard in the foreground, dated about the same vintage, was made in Kansas from a single piece of wood.*

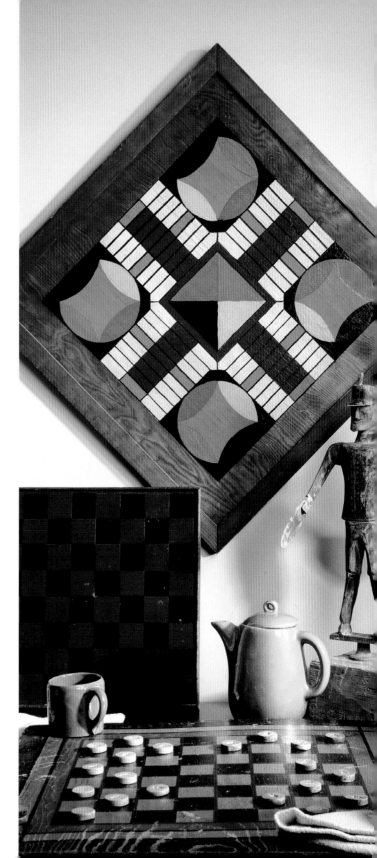

# Britain Soldiers

If it weren't for the cost, Britain Soldiers probably would have invaded more of today's toy boxes.

Britains Ltd., the most prolific and accepted toy soldier maker in the world, had its beginnings in 1845 when William Britain, Sr., the patriarch of the clan (1828–1906), began making mechanical toys. Regardless of how well-made and intricate these toys were, production costs limited their sale. It wasn't until William Britain, Jr. came upon the idea of hollow casting toy lead soldiers to broaden the firm's clientele that the company really took off.

In 1893, the first model—a mounted English Life Guard—was issued and the concept patent-

ed. The manufacture of these lead figures with their realistic anatomy continued until 1966. A reproduction of a 1936 catalog includes not only many regiments of these soldiers but also artillery, aircraft, cars, trucks, Sons of India, Armies of the World, Native Warriors and Types of the Wild West, 16th-Century Knights in Armour, Toy Tents, Hunting Series, and Zoos.

It is said that each Britain is a work of art. These finely detailed, historically accurate hand-painted replicas, made in complete regiments, were sold as sets. Some of the boxes have survived, increasing the value of the set. The Britains company trademark is always stamped on the bottom of the lead figures, which were manufactured exclusively in England. Chipped paint lowers the value of a figure.

# Raggedy Ann & Andy Dolls

With their classic triangle nose, button eyes, red yarn hair, and "I love you" painted in a heart on the chest, Raggedy Ann and Andy dolls are never boring.

Manufactured by a half dozen companies for more than eight decades, there is an amazing variety and subtle difference in designs that intrigues collectors. Early Georgene dolls, with a black outline on the nose of both Ann and Andy, are pricey, as are the additional family members, such as Beloved Belinda and Uncle Clem. The perpetual smiles on the faces of these vintage dolls are meant to illustrate kindness, generosity, friendship, and love. Smiles are different and the prints on some dresses are rare.

*Right:*

*Most dolls wear stockings with horizontal stripes.*

*Opposite:*

*The triangular noses have been worn from the two dolls in the center. The very first Raggedy Ann doll had red string hair. Black hair was introduced later.*

Stories of Raggedy Ann's origin vary slightly, but it is certain that author Johnny Gruelle (1880–1938) took out a patent for the doll in 1915. The story goes that Gruelle created Raggedy Ann for his daughter, Marcella, when she brought him a worn handmade doll she found in the attic. He drew a face on it and then marketed it along with the first of his series of Raggedy Ann Stories, published in 1918. Marcella's death at age 13 didn't stop Gruelle from continuing to write stories and market the dolls.

As a testament to their longtime popularity, Raggedy Ann and Andy were inducted into the International Toy Hall of Fame in 2002. Several craftspeople are hand making new one-of-a-kind dolls inspired by the original manufactured dolls. These may be personalized with a dated body tag and a signed hang tag, with a photograph of the doll that inspired the slightly new design.

Collector's Note: **Spotting a Good Find**
• • • • • • • • • • • • • • • • • • • • • • • • • • • • • • • • • • • •
Keep your eyes open for rare Raggedy Ann dolls with solid blue or vertical-striped stockings. Finding original hang tags on a doll, like the very scarce Silbys tags, are a collector's dream.

*Raggedy Ann and Andy may be as small as 8" or as tall at 48".*

# Sand Pails

Fond memories of lazy days at the beach are a great reason to collect old sand pails.

The charming graphics themselves help identify and date a sand pail. Ohio Art obtained a license from Disney in the 1930s before decorating its pails with Mickey Mouse. It is not clear if the same is true for an English company using the same cartoon character.

Some collectors concentrate on patriotic red, white, and blue-themed pails. Others are drawn to familiar stories like *Three Little Pigs* or the nursery rhyme, *Humpty Dumpty*. Holidays, the circus, cartoons, promotional pails, or pails of an era are collectible themes. The earliest pails were painted.

*These red, white, and blue pails were made by Wolverine, a Pennsylvania company.*

Sand pails were manufactured in many countries throughout the world, so it is impossible to say who was first. The best U.S. toymaker, Converse, was founded in 1878 in Winchendon, Massachusetts. In the early 1890s they started producing lithographed tin toys.

Since the production of sand pails was related to the printing industry, this probably happened around the same time in a number of countries. In fact, England's most famous toymaker, Chad Valley company in Harbourne, started as printers. This method was followed by offset lithography on the tin-plated steel using a rubber composition roller and, about 1930, by chromolithography, which made it possible to print more than 50 tin-plated sheets per minute.

Collector's Note: **Inspect for Rust**

Examine a sand pail in person before bidding at an auction. It might be rusty, which would lower its price.

*Some pails are marked with logos on the bottom. Some collectors augment their pails with other sand toys like sifters and watering cans.*

# Teddy Bears

Teddy bears aren't just for children anymore, just ask any arctophile. These passionate adult collectors of the huggable, lovable creatures, as they are known, are so numerous that Christie's holds two auctions a year in London devoted exclusively to the sale of Teddy bears. The Japanese collector who paid a hefty sum for an early Steiff-made bear bought his new friend a first-class airline seat for the ride home to Japan.

Early English bears have long snouts, shaped limbs, a plump body, and a hump on their backs. German bears are slimmer and American bears are even less sculptured, with thinner, straight limbs and bodies.

The nose and ears of American bears will have stitching that is not as neat and is looser than their European counterparts. The design on the metal button in the left ear of Steiff bears will help identify its period. Old bears are stiffer than later bears, as they were stuffed with wood shavings, which in the 1930s were replaced by kapok, a tropical tree. Early bears had boot-button eyes that were changed to glass eyes during the 1920s and plastic after World War II.

In addition to Steiff, desirable bears are made by Ideal, Bruin, Chad Valley, Farnell, Merrythough, and Chilton. Some early Bruin bears had musical movements in their torsos. Their battery-powered eyes might light up or the bear might growl when tilted.

*Below:*

*This collection of old and new bears represents a variety of materials including alpaca, mohair, calico, cotton, synthetic furs, wool felt, and ultra-suede.*

*Opposite:*

*These three vintage bears are not labeled. Collectors are lucky to find bears with original labels intact.*

# Tin Clockwork Cars

Wind-up cars have been a favorite of children since they first rolled onto the scene more than 100 years ago.

Tinplate, which is thin pieces of steel or iron covered with tin, is ideal for toy making as it is easy to shape and decorate. Cars and all forms of toys illustrating transportation top the list of toy collectors.

During the late 1880s European toymakers began to manufacture inexpensive tinplate toys in vast quantities. By 1900, more than a third of the tin toys made in Germany were exported to the United States. The most prominent German firms, Lehman, Marklin, and Bing, are well-known to experienced collectors. In fact, Lehman exported 90 percent of its production to the United States. The toys made by Carette, Gunthermann, and the lesser known Buchner are considered choice. Collectors shopping in Europe might find toys by the French manufacturer Fernand Martin. These were sold by street peddlers in France and rarely exported. Lithographed tin clockwork motorcars are so difficult and costly to reproduce that fakes are non-existent.

*This vintage 1900 clockwork automobile with driver was manufactured by Gunthermann, a German company. It measures 10" x 4¼" x 9". Cars with their drivers are highly prized.*

No matter how dull or worn the original paint has become, it is best to leave the paint on an antique car untouched. The small dots of the lithograph cannot be reproduced by a paintbrush for touch-up. It is the same for missing parts. Look for patent marks on antique German toys. For those made after 1890 you might find the patent number or copyright marks such as the initials O.R.G.M. standing for Deutsches Reichs Gebrauchmuster.

Because they were costly to begin with, tin clockwork cars very often have been well treated, surviving several generations as playthings.

Cars in their original boxes are worth significantly more than those without boxes. Even the condition of the box is a factor when establishing a price. The clockwork mechanism in one Ives toy was so sturdy that the car would run for an hour on a single windup.

Restored tin clockwork toys have significant value. Lehman vehicles are easy to identify as they have a logo, which is surrounded by a bell, or the full word Lehman embossed in the metal. German-made toy cars hold the record for top prices.

# Tinkertoys

You might come upon your first set of Tinkertoys at a garage or yard sale. It could be one of the first, from 1914, with the name *The Wonder Builder* on the tubular box along with drawings of a merry-go-round, Ferris wheel, or a windmill you can build.

Tinkertoys were manufactured in a large variety of sets, usually numbered and given names such as The Starter Set, Basic Beginner's Set, Superset, or Big Builder's Set.

It all started in 1913 when Charles H. Pajeau, a stone mason, and Robert Pettit, a trader, who met on a commuter train going to Chicago, joined forces to form a toy manufacturing company. Pajeau had been watching children playing with pencils and spools, taking them apart and putting them together for hours. Working on the Pythagorean principal of the progressive right triangle, he designed a wooden spool with eight holes around it and one in the center to make a cornerstone piece. Sticks that fit in the holes were all that was needed to construct all sorts of shapes.

*This donkey pull-toy, one of the many patented varieties of Tinkertoys, is pictured with its original directions.*

Early sets were of plain wood, spools, and sticks alone. In 1932 color was added to the spools, followed in 1953 by red, and then by green, yellow, and blue sticks in 1955.

Wooden figures of animals and people, electric motors, trains, and other vehicles became part of a set. Some special parts had boxes all their own. Pull-toys, the Flying Tinker propeller toy, Tip-Toe Tinker dolls, and Tilly Tinker are out there to be found. The box will tell the patent date and the number of pieces the set contained.

*Above:*

*All of the figures pull apart to become individual pieces, which fit neatly inside the original wooden box.*

*Left:*

*A wagon and goat pull-toys are choice items.*

# everyday objects

..........................................

## chapter nine

# Baby Plates

Learning begins at home. And for some tiny tots, it also starts at mealtime.

Dozens of countries throughout the world have manufactured charming baby plates decorated with familiar nursery rhymes such as *Little Bo Peep* and *Mary Had a Little Lamb* for decades. The transferware or hand-painted illustrations on the plates might carry a disciplinary or teaching theme such as the often-used ABCs around the rim. To see the difference, look at a baby plate with a magnifying glass; if it's transferware, you'll be able to see dots in the pattern. Many times the design is a combination of hand painting and transferware, which is smooth to the touch.

Marks on the back of most baby plates reveal the country of origin, the name of the maker, and an approximate date of manufacture. Wiltshaw & Robinson of Stoke on Trent, England, used a circular bird and crown mark from 1894–1927. Royal Beyrueth, Bavaria, used a distinct blue mark from 1902–1920. Paragon Porcelain, England, used a star in its back stamp from 1899–1919.

Baby plates may be made of hard-paste porcelain, sturdy white ironstone, opaque Platonite, Melamine, Carnival glass, and more. Signs of wear along with slight crazing, which refers to the cracking in the glaze, are common on these old plates.

# Cameras

Technology is great, don't get me wrong. But there's something wonderfully nostalgic about an old camera and the now-primitive need for film and processing.

Early Eastman box cameras provided a mail-in, printing, and refilling service. Owners would mail the entire camera to the factory to have the film developed, prints made, and fresh film loaded before the camera was returned to its owner. Roll film eliminated this process.

When starting a collection, decide on a specialty and then stick to your decision. Most antique wooden cameras are too expensive for the casual collector, but there are plenty of options. Decide if you want cameras that are cool to look at but use film sizes that are no longer made. It is impractical and a lot of work to cut your own.

If you want to take photographs with a vintage camera, you can have film made to fit the older varieties. Box Brownies became available in 1903 and red bellows folding cameras came on the scene a few years later.

Buy only complete cameras. If a screw is missing, an exact replacement is almost impossible to find. If a camera is in poor condition, it is a bad investment.

## Spotting a Fake

Examine the focusing ring on the front of a Zeiss lens to spot a fake. If the letter T is white instead of red and the M is a capital rather than lower case, it is not a genuine Zeiss.

# Candy Containers

You might concentrate on holiday containers, such as Halloween, Easter, or Christmas. Or you may be enchanted by rabbits, circus figures, comic characters, or animals riding in vehicles. Perhaps automatons or mechanical toys could be your theme.

Antique papier-mâché candy containers made in Germany before the first World War are rare and hard to find. If you buy a container that needs repair, consult an expert rather than attempting to repair it yourself.

*The head comes off the tall papier-mâché rabbit pushing the wheelbarrow to reveal a cavity full of candy. The eggs, which are also candy containers, are decorated with chromolithographs and trimmed with paper lace. All were made in Germany before World War I.*

The production of candy containers became a cottage industry after its introduction in 1819 in Sonneberg, Thuringa, the then toy-making center in southeastern Germany and the world. Individual artisans made candy containers in their homes in the countless tiny villages in the forests of Thuringa. Most families could produce 12–15 pieces per week. The husband would prepare the plaster mold and form the container, and then his wife and children would paint and decorate both parts of the container, giving special attention to the faces.

Antique candy containers have a mellow look and display a personality and artistry not found in the mass-produced reproductions.

*Above:*

*German manufacturers catered to America's infatuation with the circus by exporting large quantities of candy containers featuring circus characters such as these five clowns.*

*Opposite:*

*The larger turkeys may have been part of a store display, while the smaller papier-mâché turkeys were meant to be enjoyed in homes.*

# Cocktail Shakers

Few beverage accessories are as swanky as the cocktail shaker.

Thanks to the grand renaissance of the martini, a mood reminiscent of the sophisticated era of the glamorous cocktail party, a new generation of young collectors is on the rise, making barware a trendy collectible.

Silver-plate, chrome, aluminum, glass, or nickel-plate were commonly used materials to make shakers in a myriad of forms, including skyscrapers, penguins, bowling pins, roosters, zeppelins, hour glasses, and other icons of the period, along with the traditional cylinder shapes. Many were patented and given names by the manufacturer.

*Right:*

*The c. 1928 Wallace Brothers hand-hammered silver rooster (right) is a choice piece. The 1929 rooster (center) has a silver-over-brass head.*

*Opposite:*

*Chrome barware, such as this Keystone Ware ice bucket with its Bakelite knob and the teapot-style shaker are Art Deco.*

The 1930s Blue Moon and Blue Doric shakers by Chase are sought after by collectors, and copies of the original patents are available.

If you are new to the world of barware and budget is a restraint, look for glass shakers of the 1950s and 1960s at flea markets, antique malls, yard sales, and local antique shops. Some craftspersons of today are making new shakers inspired by the designs of the Art Deco era.

## Spotting a Fake

Reproductions of the famous Napier Penguin shaker, originally engraved Made in India, are now marked with a paper label, making them easier to pass off as originals. Most reproductions are advertised honestly and sold as new pieces.

*Figural shakers like the 1920s silver-plate English tank and German design windmill from the same era along with the 1950s robot are important vintage pieces.*

# Egg Cups

The humble egg must have held great prominence on the breakfast table to warrant its own cup.

Egg cups date back to Roman times, when eggs were first boiled. They eventually re-emerged and they were widely used during the Victorian period. Most were ceramic, but egg cups have also been made of wood, glass, metal, and Jadeite.

*These Depression-era ceramic egg cups might have come from a grandmother's cupboard. Eggs were usually eaten right from the shell, but could be emptied into the larger side of the cup.*

Although the practice of perching your egg in a cup may be all but extinct, there are thousands of egg cups decades old, waiting to be discovered and appreciated by collectors. Egg cups can be found in the shape of a rooster, hen, bunny, or many other fanciful shapes in every color of the rainbow. Materials include glass, silver, alabaster, marble, plastic, aluminum, pottery, and porcelain.

Collector's Note:
**A Royal Order**
• • • • • • • • • • • • • • • • • • • • • • •
Louis XV in France loved his boiled eggs so much that he commissioned his court jewelers to design egg cups exclusively for his use.

*Left:*

*These ceramic egg cups are decorated with a transferware pattern.*

*Opposite:*

*The translucent green cups are Depression-era Jadeite. The hand-painted cup on the left is from Japan.*

# Horse Trophies

Engraved trophies are reminders of equestrian victories, recalling mankind's long romance with the horse.

So many fabulous sterling silver trophies are out there, such as the ornate 1901 Jockey Cup by James Gerrard, hallmarked London, 1893, that was awarded for a race at the Newmarket Raceway in Newmarket, England.

The stunning sterling silver cup, called the Brooking Corinthian Cup, was awarded to the winner on August 8, 1881, at New South Wales.

A rare 1878 steeplechase trophy from New Zealand has the winner's time stamped on the bottom along with the name of the manufacturer.

*Right:*

*Pictured is the top of the Red Coat Farm trophy awarded for a hunter-class competition at Liberty Farms in Lake Forest, Illinois.*

*Opposite:*

*Related treasures such as antique programs and photographs augment the trophies.*

Horse trophies as we know them today have been awarded for about 150 years. Marvelous antique ornate trophies from the late 19th century command high prices. Think not only of the traditional cups but of silver Revere bowls, goblets, plates, platters, stirrup cups, horse figures, mint julep cups, and salts and peppers. There are 523 horse trophies on display at the International Museum of the Horse in Lexington, Kentucky.

Collector's Note:
**Surviving Pieces**
........................
Ornate pre-1900 silver trophies from England, Australia, New South Wales, and New Zealand are especially rare because so many were melted for the silver during hard times.

*The silver stirrup cup with a fox head is reminiscent of a fox hunt. The horn used by the huntsmen to call the hound is brass and silver.*

# Inkwells

No matter how thrilling it might be to find an antique inkwell at a flea market or garage sale, these venues are slim pickings. Your odds of finding collectible inkwells are far greater at a specialty collectibles show or an online auction site.

Ornate inkwells have been made in every conceivable material in an infinite number of designs. Some inkwells depict legends and tales of a country. There are figural inkwells representing the mythical Greek figure of Poseidon, god of the sea. Others portray the American statesman Benjamin Franklin, a humorous English barrister, with the wells cleverly hidden. Figural shapes were costly, probably limiting their clientele to the upper classes.

*Butterfly designs decorate a Limoges brass-based inkwell, which once enhanced the writing desk of a 19th-century French lady.*

The original, simpler inkwell was called a standish. It was used by paid scribes in the 16th century. Later it became an elaborate work of art culminating in Victorian times. Today, prices for gold and silver inkwells have zoomed out of sight.

Collector's Note:
## A Simple Replacement
After 4,500 years of use in all literate nations, inkwells have disappeared from the scene after having been replaced by ball-point pens.

*Left:*

*The Victorians' interest in nature is revealed in these animal and bird stands.*

*Opposite:*

*Porcelain, brass, and bronze inkwells are choice 19th-century pieces.*

# Lady Head Vases

Judging by the number of surviving pieces, these beauties must have been in great demand at their height of production. About 10,000 different varieties of Lady Head Vases were produced during their heyday, from the 1940s through the 1970s, resulting in an untapped supply for today's head hunter to discover.

These shapely vases were used by floral designers around the world, especially in Japan, where the largest number was made. Companies such as Napco and Enarco dated and labeled their products, and also included the model number. California artist Betty Lou Nichols had a line all her own.

Some collectors specialize in vases by Nichols, and experienced collectors say they can recognize a Nichols vase by its style. Some of the heavier ceramic Glamour Girl vases had the name imprinted in the ceramic material, while others were imprinted simply with U.S.A.

*Top:*

*These demure women all have false eyelashes.*

*Opposite:*

*Many Lady Head Vases, grouped by size and displayed on these shelves, wear hats, which is preferred by collectors.*

## Collector's Note: **Larger Than Life**

Most collectors prefer detailed painting with realistic features, pearl earrings, and perhaps a bouffant hairdo. Celebrity figures, including Marilyn Monroe, Lucille Ball, Carmen Miranda, and Jackie O, command the highest prices.

# Paperweights

You don't have to know a lot about paperweights to collect them.

There may be different means to the madness but the most common is type collecting. This includes at least one example of each: millefiori, thin cross sections of glass canes usually resembling little flowers; lampwork, featuring objects such as flowers, butterflies, fruit, and animals made by shaping colored glass with a gas burner; and sulphide, a ceramic portrait plaque or medallion encased in glass.

Between 1845 and 1860, thousands of paperweights were created in one of the French glass factories, Baccarat, St. Louis, or Clichy. They not only held down papers on a desk in a breezy office but were also admired for their aesthetics. The tiny slices of different-colored glass rods were set in a mold and covered with clear glass, making an infinite variety of designs possible.

After this classic period came to an end, paperweight manufacturing was nearly forgotten until it blossomed again in the 1950s and continues today. Contemporary pieces give collectors the opportunity to collect these lovely art glass items at affordable prices.

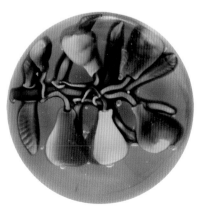

# Salt & Pepper Shakers

Salt and pepper shakers have been collected ever since they replaced the Victorian era's open salt dish and tiny spoon.

As the use of all types of ceramics soared, so did the production of these tiny treasures in many countries, including Japan, China, Korea, Taiwan, and the United States.

To begin your hunt, familiarize yourself with shaker terminology. You should know that *anthros* are shakers that are not human shapes, but have human faces, while *go-togethers* are shakers that are not identical but have a common theme. *Hangers* are shakers that hang off a base. *Kissers* look like they are kissing. With *nesters*, one shaker fits into an indentation in the other. And then there are *stackers*, where one fits on top of the other.

*Above:*

*The ceramic camel is a hanger shaker set. The salt and pepper are housed in the bags hanging on the camel. Birds, faces, plants, and animals are common themes.*

*Opposite:*

*The marked shakers in this group are labeled Japan.*

# Syrup Pitchers

Whether they were called griddle cakes, pancakes, or flapjacks, these breakfast favorites were never served alone.

Syrup pitchers were usually filled with a sweet maple syrup. Small vessels for this special purpose began their life in the middle of the 19th century, when the formal Victorian breakfast table was enhanced with a *syrup* made of silver, or pressed or blown glass. Simpler tables used ironstone pitchers, both unadorned and embossed with intricate designs. Patents were obtained for most.

Today's collector will find syrups from the 1930s to be more plentiful and affordable. From the 1930s through the 1950s, numerous colored-glass pitchers were manufactured, usually with metal lids and thumb mecha-nisms. Thousands of plain-glass pitchers featured colorful Bakelite plastic lids and handles.

Collectors covet yellow plastic lids, with red running a close second. One may wonder what happened to the 100,000 pieces the U.S. Army ordered at the beginning of World War II. No doubt some have become part of a collector's treasure trove.

*Above:*

*Green Depression-era glass syrups are a favorite with collectors.*

*Opposite:*

*Milk glass pitchers from the early 20th century are embossed with intricate patterns.*

# Teapots

Tea is the most widely consumed beverage in the world, so it seems only fitting to honor the soothing drink by collecting the teapot.

Enchanting and diverse examples come from many countries including China, Japan, England, and the United States. The secret of a well-made teapot is simple: After covering a pot with a glaze, it is fired in an outdoor kiln and then buried in straw or sawdust or left to cool. This technique contributes to the individuality of each finished piece.

The art of teapot-making is more than 500 years old. The earliest examples of teapots came from the Ming Dynasty in China (1368–1644). They are prized for their fine texture, thin walls, and colors ranging from light buff to deep maroon.

In Japan, artist Sen Rikyn (1522–1591) was at the forefront of artistic teapot designs. Teapots with themes of nature were prized. The Japanese imported Chinese potters to teach them potting methods. The art of teapot-making spread globally and continues today.

*Left:*

*Ceramic artist Patrick Horsley created this blue teapot with a trumpeting spout. It is aptly called an elephantine design.*

*Opposite:*

*Collected by instinct rather than for their market value, the diverse teapots lining the glass shelves form a cohesive group.*

# Traveler's Clocks

The classic carriage clock was well-traveled, tagging along on many train and carriage rides between 1860 and 1900.

The first authentic carriage clocks were made in Paris at the beginning of the 19th century by Abraham-Louis Breguet (1747–1823). His complex design was considered an incredible feat of workmanship. It featured hours, minutes, seconds, phases of the moon, an alarm, an up-and-down dial showing the state of the wind, regulator dial with the day, date, month, year, temperature, and more.

Carriage clocks were simplified and made in France by L'Epee, Francoise Margaine, Japy Freres, and Henry Jacot. In England, Elkington & Company, Richard & Company, Hunt & Roskell, and Aubert & Klaftenberger joined the group. In the United States, Eli Terry first mass-produced clocks. He was followed by Cauncey Jerrome, the New Haven Clock Company, Seth Thomas, and others.

Most collectors think of the carriage clock as one with its mechanism enclosed in a brass case with windows to display the works, a fold-down handle, and most likely a white enamel face with black lettering. There can be a vast difference in quality, size, housing, and time-striking features. Chimes, gongs, or bells, for example, can be repeating or non-repeating.

*Right and Opposite:*
*These handsome brass carriage clocks awakened continental travelers in the late 19th century.*

# About the Author

Jessie Walker is a renowned international assignment and stock photographer who devotes much of her time to photographing homes, gardens, and collections for publication in national magazines.

She has photographed on assignment throughout the United States and in England, France, Germany, and Norway. Her photography of people and places in India, Thailand, and Myanmar (Burma) has become part of corporate design. Her photography has been the subject of one-person shows at the Chicago Press Club, the Chicago Athletic Club, Ruth Volid Gallery, and the Zenith Corporate headquarters. Jessie's work is part of the permanent collection of the Museum of Contemporary Photography, Chicago. The museum named her the best photographer of interiors in the area and honored her in a special exhibition, *Target Market*.

Her photography has been published in more than 130 hardcover books. She is the author of *Jessie Walker's Country Decorating* (© 2004 Sterling Publishing Co., Inc.) and *Country Living Collectibles—Rabbits* (© 1996 William Morrow & Company, Inc.).

Even though Jessie holds both bachelor's and master's degrees in journalism with special research in the legibility of type faces, her true love is photography. She is a member of the American Society of Media Photographers. Jessie lives in Glencoe, Illinois, with her husband, Arthur Griggs.

# Sources

Association of Game and Puzzle Collectors
www.agpc.org

Blue & White Pottery Club
www.blueandwhitepottery.org

Bubble Gum and Candy Wrappers Association
www.TheWrapperMagazine.com

Candy Containers Collectors Club of America
www.candycontainer.org

Decoys
*Decoy Magazine*
www.decoymag.com

The Ephemera Society of America
www.ephemerasociety.org

Fishing Lures
The Worldwide Bass Fishing Club

Flower Frogs
*Flower Frogs for the Collector* by Bonnie Bull

Game Boards
*Association of Game & Puzzle Collectors*
www.agpc.org

International Match Safe Association
www.matchsafe.org

International Society of Antique Scale Collectors
www.isasc.org

Lady Head Vases
*The Encyclopedia of Head Vases* by Kathleen Cole

National Association of Watch and Clock Collectors
www.nawcc.org

National Graniteware Society
www.graniteware.org
*The Collectors' Encyclopedia of Graniteware* by Helen Greguires

National Milk Glass Collectors Society
www.nmgcs.org

National Novelty Salt & Pepper Shakers Club
www.saltandpepperclub.com

Raggedy Ann and Andy Dolls
*Rags Magazine*
www.rankinpublishing.com

Sand Pails
*Sand Pail Encyclopedia: A Complete Value Guide for Tin-litho Sand Toys* by Karen Homan and Sally Minick

Society of Inkwell Collectors
www.soic.com

Tea Leaf Club International
www.tealeafclub.com

Tinkertoys
*The Collectors Guide to Tinker Toys* by Craig Strange

Wakefield Wicker Society
www.wakefield.org/wicker

# Metric Equivalency Charts

## inches to millimeters and centimeters

| inches | mm | cm | inches | cm | inches | cm |
|---|---|---|---|---|---|---|
| ⅛ | 3 | 0.3 | 9 | 22.9 | 30 | 76.2 |
| ¼ | 6 | 0.6 | 10 | 25.4 | 31 | 78.7 |
| ⅜ | 9 | 1.0 | 11 | 27.9 | 32 | 81.3 |
| ½ | 13 | 1.3 | 12 | 30.5 | 33 | 83.8 |
| ⅝ | 16 | 1.6 | 13 | 33.0 | 34 | 86.4 |
| ¾ | 19 | 1.9 | 14 | 35.6 | 35 | 88.9 |
| ⅞ | 22 | 2.2 | 15 | 38.1 | 36 | 91.4 |
| 1 | 25 | 2.5 | 16 | 40.6 | 37 | 94.0 |
| 1¼ | 32 | 3.2 | 17 | 43.2 | 38 | 96.5 |
| 1½ | 38 | 3.8 | 18 | 45.7 | 39 | 99.1 |
| 1¾ | 44 | 4.4 | 19 | 48.3 | 40 | 101.6 |
| 2 | 51 | 5.1 | 20 | 50.8 | 41 | 104.1 |
| 2½ | 64 | 6.4 | 21 | 53.3 | 42 | 106.7 |
| 3 | 76 | 7.6 | 22 | 55.9 | 43 | 109.2 |
| 3½ | 89 | 8.9 | 23 | 58.4 | 44 | 111.8 |
| 4 | 102 | 10.2 | 24 | 61.0 | 45 | 114.3 |
| 4½ | 114 | 11.4 | 25 | 63.5 | 46 | 116.8 |
| 5 | 127 | 12.7 | 26 | 66.0 | 47 | 119.4 |
| 6 | 152 | 15.2 | 27 | 68.6 | 48 | 121.9 |
| 7 | 178 | 17.8 | 28 | 71.1 | 49 | 124.5 |
| 8 | 203 | 20.3 | 29 | 73.7 | 50 | 127.0 |

## yards to meters

| yards | meters | yards | meters | yards | meters | yards | meters | yards | meters |
|---|---|---|---|---|---|---|---|---|---|
| ⅛ | 0.11 | 2⅛ | 1.94 | 4⅛ | 3.77 | 6⅛ | 5.60 | 8⅛ | 7.43 |
| ¼ | 0.23 | 2¼ | 2.06 | 4¼ | 3.89 | 6¼ | 5.72 | 8¼ | 7.54 |
| ⅜ | 0.34 | 2⅜ | 2.17 | 4⅜ | 4.00 | 6⅜ | 5.83 | 8⅜ | 7.66 |
| ½ | 0.46 | 2½ | 2.29 | 4½ | 4.11 | 6½ | 5.94 | 8½ | 7.77 |
| ⅝ | 0.57 | 2⅝ | 2.40 | 4⅝ | 4.23 | 6⅝ | 6.06 | 8⅝ | 7.89 |
| ¾ | 0.69 | 2¾ | 2.51 | 4¾ | 4.34 | 6¾ | 6.17 | 8¾ | 8.00 |
| ⅞ | 0.80 | 2⅞ | 2.63 | 4⅞ | 4.46 | 6⅞ | 6.29 | 8⅞ | 8.12 |
| 1 | 0.91 | 3 | 2.74 | 5 | 4.57 | 7 | 6.40 | 9 | 8.23 |
| 1⅛ | 1.03 | 3⅛ | 2.86 | 5⅛ | 4.69 | 7⅛ | 6.52 | 9⅛ | 8.34 |
| 1¼ | 1.14 | 3¼ | 2.97 | 5¼ | 4.80 | 7¼ | 6.63 | 9¼ | 8.46 |
| 1⅜ | 1.26 | 3⅜ | 3.09 | 5⅜ | 4.91 | 7⅜ | 6.74 | 9⅜ | 8.57 |
| 1½ | 1.37 | 3½ | 3.20 | 5½ | 5.03 | 7½ | 6.86 | 9½ | 8.69 |
| 1⅝ | 1.49 | 3⅝ | 3.31 | 5⅝ | 5.14 | 7⅝ | 6.97 | 9⅝ | 8.80 |
| 1¾ | 1.60 | 3¾ | 3.43 | 5¾ | 5.26 | 7¾ | 7.09 | 9¾ | 8.92 |
| 1⅞ | 1.71 | 3⅞ | 3.54 | 5⅞ | 5.37 | 7⅞ | 7.20 | 9⅞ | 9.03 |
| 2 | 1.83 | 4 | 3.66 | 6 | 5.49 | 8 | 7.32 | 10 | 9.14 |

# Acknowledgments

## Collectors

## Antique Dealers

## Artisans

# Index